STORY

**A Father's Shares a
Son's Struggle with
Bipolar, Substance,
Suicide and Faith**

Advantage
INSPIRATIONAL™

KEN DIGNAN

Ryan's Story by Ken Dignan
Copyright © 2005 by Kenneth M. Dignan
All Rights Reserved.
ISBN: 1-59755-021-3

Published by: *ADVANTAGE BOOKS*™
www.advbooks.com

All Scripture quotations, unless indicated, are taken from the Holy Bible New International Version (NIV). Copyright 1973, 1978, 1984 by International Bible Society. Used by permission of Zondervan Publishing House. All rights reserved.

Library of Congress Control Number: 2005933420

First Printing: November 2005

04 05 06 07 08 09 10   9 8 7 6 5 4 3 2

Printed in the United States of America

Table of Contents

Acknowledgements

This book began as a journal. It brought me some relief to begin writing down my thoughts and feelings the day after the suicidal death of my 20-year-old son Ryan. It felt therapeutic and comforting to sit at the keyboard and put down my wide range of feelings.

For the first number of months I wrote something every night. Sometimes I would go on for hours not being able to sleep anyway. I am very grateful to family and friends who shared a number of thoughts about my son that are included in this book.

I will be forever grateful to the members of Eagle Rock Community Church where I serve as a pastor. Their love, compassion, support and understanding were and have been phenomenal.

It was a lifesaver to have a friend recommend to my wife and I a ministry called LOSS (Loving Outreach to Survivors of Suicide) an outreach from the Catholic Charities of the Archdiocese of Chicago and founder Father Charles Rubey. He graciously met with us personally and shared compassionately with us in our grief. We also participated in a ten-week LOSS support group, just weeks after Ryan's death that was very beneficial.

I am grateful for the feedback and editorial assistance of Sally E. Stuart, author of the annual Christian Writers Market Guide, Karyn Stone of Advantage Books and my friend, Jon Koys. Special thanks go to Debbie Maish who spent many hours typing several edits.

Many helpful websites and books on bipolar and suicide provided a wealth of information as I dug in deeper to understand my son's disorder. They are referenced in the back pages of this book.

Where would I be in all that transpired without the love and support of my parents, my brothers and sisters, and my wife's family?

As loving parents, my wife and I experienced, and continue to experience, this journey of pain, grief and healing. Her grace, compassion, kindness and love have been a real blessing to me as we both suffer this grief together. My son Andrew and his wife Jodi, who Ryan loved as a sister, Patrick and Britt, miss Ryan along-side of us, filling in the vacuum he left, with their love.

Of course, I will forever love and appreciate my dear son, Ryan Lee Dignan, born September 15, 1982 and entering heaven December 14, 2002. It was his love for life, family, friends, people, music, sports and God that has driven me to write this book.

It is my desire to do anything I can to keep his memory alive and share everything he went through as he battled to survive in the midst of unbelievable odds and challenges. He was extremely special and precious to us. Thank you, Ryan for being you. We'll be together again someday.

Foreword

Grief is a journey that takes its participants over a rocky path with many potholes and obstacles. The journey never ends but the path does get smoother as the travelers become more comfortable with the pain that accompanies them. When a person's death is a suicide there are unique issues that impact surviving family and friends. Ken and Joni Dignan have been on this journey since their son, Ryan, found life too painful to handle and took things into his own hands. His death was a dramatic statement that clearly said, "I have run out of steam. I can no longer do this." Not the result of moral turpitude or weakness. Ryan's death resulted from the struggles he had with a mood disorder called bipolar.

This book is all about Ryan and the impact his death had on his family. Suicide is different from other forms of death. If he had been hit by a car, contracted a lethal illness or drowned, the cause of death would be clear. With suicide there are not clear-cut reasons as to why Ryan died. Survivors struggle with these intangibles and ultimately are forced to face living with the unknown. One thing we know is that a mood disorder can be a very lethal illness.

This book is one family's story about the impact of their loved ones battle with bipolar and subsequent suicide. There are countless other families who have similar stories. The characters change but the plot is often the same.

Onlookers wonder what could have been so wrong with a person who attempts a suicide or what could have been so wrong with that family. There is nothing wrong with the person or with the family. People don't ask that question if someone dies from cancer or heart disease.

Suicide results from a disease that affects the mind and the soul. As you read this book, hopefully you will gain insight into the unknown world of mood disorders and develop understanding towards one who found life so painful that he would instead choose death.

We should not judge anyone nor should we come to false conclusions or erroneous reasons as to why someone takes his or her life. We commend these souls to a loving God and pray that their loved ones will turn to Him to find peace.

Rev. Charles T. Rubey
Founder of LOSS
(Loving Outreach to Survivors of Suicide)
The Catholic Charities of the Archdiocese of Chicago

Introduction

This book is dedicated to the memory of my son, Ryan. It chronicles a difficult and dark time in the life of a unique and wonderful human being. He manifested symptoms of bipolar disorder around the age of sixteen, but it went undiagnosed until he was seventeen. Neither Ryan nor I knew much about the disorder. As we were thrust into that stark, cold reality of a psychological disorder, we attempted to learn as much as we could to try to overcome its effects on our son.

Ryan's story provides a look at how bipolar drastically alters the life of any individual who has it. It also shows the profound effect it has on the family members. No one really knows the nightmare of living with "manic-depression" unless you or a family member is diagnosed with it.

This story is shared from my perspective as a father. Our family is composed of my wife, Joni, and our four sons. These are my reflections as I saw and felt them. It focuses on many of the problems Ryan experienced as a teenager. Let it be known there are more good memories and wonderful family times we had with our son, than the negative situations chronicled in this writing.

The purpose of this book is to show a firsthand account of a father, who saw one of his children trapped in the vicious cycle of a chemical imbalance. This problem, referred to as bipolar disorder contributed to my son's suicide.

I began writing down my thoughts and feelings about Ryan's and our experiences the last five years of his life. I kept writing for many months and years. Eventually they became, "RYAN'S STORY."

I believe I did everything possible to help my son. I felt it was my God-given call to get Ryan through this terrible thing called bipolar. I consider this book a labor of love. I hope these contents will keep Ryan's memory alive, so many can see what a unique and wonderful person he was.

Ryan's mother, Joni, along with our faith in God, was the glue that held us all together. Her loving care, patience, and unending persistence to do whatever it took to help our son was remarkable. I will never forget the way she gave of herself. We know Ryan looks down from heaven and shares my appreciation for his mother.

Ryan's three brothers tried to help him deal with his bipolar and the substance abuse to which it led. Kids are kids and there were times when they would get upset at one another and bicker and fight. But these brothers did all they could to understand and come to grips with the problems and changes their sibling was going through. They loved him and were turned upside down by the shock of his suicide.

In this book, I open the door of our home for you to look into and see what a family goes through when faced with the terrible disorder called bipolar. As you read this story, you can see our reaction to Ryan's diagnosis of bipolar disorder. You will get a glimpse of how we struggled to help our son deal with this nightmare, and what the results of that struggle were.

I want to help parents, spouses, children, relatives, and friends gain a better understanding of bipolar disorder and how to help a loved one who has it. I also hope to share insights into mood disorders and substance abuse with doctors, psychiatrists, psychologists, and counselors involved in these areas of mental health.

Another goal of this book is to raise public awareness of this disorder to pursue more tax dollars and private donations for greater research into mental illness, substance abuse and suicide prevention.

I desire to unmask the ugly head of suicide among those with bipolar. I am driven to encourage anyone who is thinking about suicide to realize you do not have to take that desperate and final act. There is help and hope for you. Your loved ones and friends will never be the same if you choose to end your pain and confusion by suicide. Although our faith in God sustains us, the underlying current of loss remains.

I never dreamt that my son would take his own life. I realized it was a possibility. I knew that many who have bipolar try to commit suicide, but I believed we were doing everything possible to prevent Ryan from doing so.

I cannot imagine the pain that caused my son to choose this desperate way to end his life. It is hard to conceive what would have convinced him that ending his earthly life was the only way out. His entire family and friends grieve our loss. The pain will never go away. Though many individuals with bipolar can successfully deal with and treat this disorder, there is a handful that cannot. Those who attempt to or actually commit suicide have a mysterious darkness and screaming pain that specialists in the field of medicine and psychiatry have yet to predict, prevent and successfully treat.

With millions struggling from mental disorders, Ryan's chronicle should help you gain more compassion and understanding for anyone who is afflicted with bipolar disorder.

Rev. Kenneth M. Dignan, ThD.

Chapter One

A Universe Away

On a warm Saturday in August of 2000, our family was celebrating a weekend reunion. My parents, all of my siblings and their spouses were meeting at a fine restaurant in suburban Chicago to eat dinner. While we were there we all had a great time of food and fellowship together. We laughed and reminisced as is the custom at such gatherings.

My wife Joni and I went to sleep that night, without knowing where our seventeen-year-old son Ryan was, a frequent occurrence at our house. As usual he was told to be home by midnight, but he often broke curfew, even though he realized there would be unpleasant consequences. It was apparent that he would rather suffer any disciplinary action than miss one moment with his friends. Close to midnight, the phone rang, waking me out of a deep sleep.

The words dreaded by every parent leapt across the receiver, "This is the Orland Park Police Department. Your son Ryan has been in an automobile accident and we have him in an ambulance and need to take him to the hospital. He drove your car into a park and crashed it into a port-o-potty, a swing set and teeter-totter. Your car is presently suspended on a pole. The good news is that no one was in the park.

When we arrived on the scene your son was standing on the hood of the car begging us to shoot him and to kill him. He told us to put him out of his misery. The officers on the site subdued him, and brought him to the police station. We held him here until an ambulance could arrive."

The police officer then told us that they were taking him to the local hospital and that one of his parents should meet them there. We will always be grateful to the Orland Park policemen who recognized that this was a teen in trouble and not just a rebellious kid who should be put in jail.

When we got to the hospital, we gave them our insurance card and a brief medical history for Ryan. We then rushed into the emergency room where we found our son pleading at the top of his lungs that he wanted to get out of the hospital! He had to be restrained and forced to give blood and urine for an analysis.

The tests showed a blood alcohol level of .26 (.08 being the legal limit) and in addition to that, he had a large amount of vicodin, a pain killer, in his system. We would later discover he had indulged in vodka and vicodin cocktails the ingredients of which are glasses of vodka, which are followed by snorting crushed vicodin.

That night in the emergency room was endless for us. Whenever we tried to talk to him, he would become enraged. He wanted to go home but we would not sign him out. Things got so bad the staff asked us to remain in a closed waiting room in the emergency room, and from there, we could hear Ryan's furious pleadings to "get me out of here."

When morning finally came, we stumbled home, all

the while wondering what was so terribly wrong with our son. Why was he doing this? Why did he want to die?

Why was he driven to self-destruction? Why was he so determined to end it all? These questions and so many more had no answers, as we desperately wanted to get to the bottom of Ryan's trouble.

The hospital said they were not equipped to keep someone who would have to be restrained, so he was transferred to a psychiatric hospital that specialized in helping troubled teenagers with psychological and/or substance abuse problems.

Ryan underwent ten days of treatment with various medications, group therapy, psychological testing with doctors, psychiatrists and social workers. We also had numerous family sessions with all of our children present and separate times with just Joni, Ryan, me and the therapists.

When the test results came back, the doctor told us that the findings pointed to bipolar disorder, formerly known as "manic-depression." He would need to be placed on medications and have regular therapy sessions with a counselor and psychiatrist. Here was our seventeen-year-old son in a psychiatric hospital having to be on medicine so he could function on a daily basis as a human being. What happened to our old Ryan? How had it come to this?

A Strong-willed Child and Stubborn Perfectionist

I have a special spot in my heart for Ryan. Our third child had an unbelievable zest for life. As a small child he was energetic, inquisitive, imaginative and sensitive. Yet he was very strong willed. It was hard to get him to do anything he did not want to do. He had a stubborn way of outlasting us in any power struggle. We read all the parenting books on the subject, especially the ones by Dr. James Dobson (founder of Focus on the Family), "The Strong Willed Child" and "Dare to Discipline." (1) They were very helpful but posed a huge challenge as we continued to sharpen our parenting skills.

As an example of his extremely strong willed nature, let me share this experience. When Ryan was two years old, our family drove to Wisconsin for my brother Leo's wedding. On the way back to Chicago, we stopped at a Howard Johnson's to eat. Ryan did not want to go in. Remember, he was two. We finally carried him in and sat him in a high chair, kicking and screaming. Within a few minutes, he escaped from his high chair and ran into the hotel lobby still crying. My wife took his arm and swatted him on the butt. A woman in the lobby gave her a dirty look and muttered something about child abuse. Ryan never gave in. Joni had to take him on a walk around the premises to calm him down. The result of our meal was severe indigestion.

His strong will never let up. He had a knack for getting into everything. Having two older brothers, I am sure he felt the need to compete. Yet, we like to refer to him as our own "Huckleberry Finn." If there was a river, he would swim it, if there was a mountain, he would scale it, if there was a fight, he would win it.

Cherish Every Moment
When your children are born you look at them with awe

and amazement. You want the best for them. You dream, hope and pray they will live successful, happy and fulfilling lives.

You exclaim over their first step, their first words and their first birthday. You celebrate milestones such as their first tooth, first day at school and their first crayon drawing.

You cherish every moment with your children. None of us wants to think our kids may get a terrible disease, suffer a tragic accident or pass away at an early age.

If anyone was destined for something big it was Ryan. He lived large. One summer my wife took the kids up to Minneapolis to see her family. They stopped at the Fort McCoy military base outside Sparta, Wisconsin and were excited to get out of the car after a long drive. There were large bluffs that went up fifty to one hundred feet or so. Ryan, the adventurer, convinced one of his brothers to climb the rock hills with him.

Ryan kept going, higher and higher. His brother wisely stopped and warned him to do the same, but on he went. Eventually he got so high he realized there was not enough footing to find his way back down safely. He began to yell for help. His mother and brother tried to coax him down, but to no avail and soon went to look for any assistance available.

Fortunately they found a forest ranger who knew what to do. He was rescued safely and eventually got down to solid ground. That was Ryan. He was always looking for newer and bigger challenges. He was now facing the biggest challenge of his young life.

Lion in a Cage

Upon hearing the diagnosis of bipolar, Ryan tried

various medications. His psychiatrists and counselors tried to help but to no avail. One tell-tale sign of his trauma was his restlessness. Few diversions such as watching a movie, driving a car and listening to music, rendered his only peace. He would often pace around the house like a caged lion.

I saw panic, fear; depression and hopelessness grip this once fearless, now troubled young man's heart. He had been such a "normal" kid up until now.

No One Understands

He believed that if he had a physical deformity people could at least visually see his problem instead of placing judgment upon his actions. Ryan often told me he would rather have gotten polio than bipolar. When I was a fourteen-month old child, I contracted the polio virus in 1952, three years before the polio virus vaccine, in 1955.

He would often say to us, "You don't understand how I feel." And we would reply, "We know son, but we are trying."

He asked his mother once, "Am I going to be like this for the rest of my life?" She replied, "With medication, counseling and avoiding substance abuse, you should be able to live a normal life." Yet, after Ryan was diagnosed with bipolar, nothing ever seemed normal again and you will see the complete story unfold in the pages to follow.

Witnessing a Slow Death

As a teenager, this young man was being attacked with a disease that began to rob him of his own life. It seemed as though we were watching our son die a slow death. Our whole family was working desperately to save Ryan.

"Bipolar disorder affects 1 to 2 ½ percent of the population, even the famous. (Robin Williams, Drew Carey, Patty Duke, Ernest Hemingway, Abraham Lincoln, to name a few) The stigma however, remains strong in the minds of the public and even our own families. Those who suffer from bipolar disorder can feel lonely, judged, and different as if there is no hope for them or their lives." (2)

Never Saw It Coming

There was no apparent indication that Ryan may have been manic-depressive during his childhood years. He seemed like a happy, well adjusted, above average student, ranking in the top percentile of his class in the large Chicago-area high school of almost four thousand students.

Sports were a big part of his life. In junior high, he played on the basketball team. In high school, he competed in baseball, football and wrestling. Ryan tackled everything with boundless effort. As a driven perfectionist, he wanted to be the best in whatever he did, whether it was his studies, sports or at church. He especially loved the outdoors. How could a kid so strong, handsome, smart, friendly, popular and caring become such a tormented person?

Some of the psychiatrists who treated our son told us a person who has bipolar usually exhibits latent symptoms, often unnoticed in childhood. We noticed, as he grew up he would have many temper tantrums and a firm strong-will, coupled with stubbornness and rebellion. But never did we consider, with any of these symptoms, the possibility of bipolar disorder.

Seeing the tumult our son was experiencing in his mid-teens, we could not avoid the dual diagnosis of bipolar disorder and substance abuse. No other answers explained his behavior. As I researched and studied about the symptoms of bipolar disorder, coupled with my son's self-medication with alcohol and drugs, I could see the handwriting on the wall.

Drawn to Barret Robbins

At the time of writing this chapter I was drawn to the experience of Barret Robbins. He was a professional football player for the Oakland Raiders. A little over a month after my son died I read the headlines about Barret.

He did not show up for the Superbowl XXXVII game with the Oakland Raiders versus the Tampa Bay Buccaneers. His life was out of control and he spent a lot of time partying and wound up wandering around in Tijuana not knowing where was.

Shortly after the Super Bowl of 2003, I saw Barret Robbins on ESPN during a national sports television program. He was sharing in-depth, with an interviewer, about the nightmare that led him into alcoholism, depression, and manic episodes. The woman conducting the interview said, "I don't know what bipolar disorder feels like. Can you describe it to me?" Barrett replied, "It is like driving down the expressway in thick traffic, speeding along, when all of a sudden your gas pedal and brakes don't work and your steering wheel falls off. You feel out of control."

The interviewer then asked if he still had a job with the Raiders. He said, "Coach Callahan told the team if they wanted me I could stay. If they didn't I'd have to leave. He went on to say, "I can accept whatever my teammates decide. I'll still work real hard to get ready for summer camp." (3)

If Barret struggled with diabetes or cancer, I am sure there would have been overwhelming support for his recovery, both from fans and friends. He would be encouraged to stay on the team as long as he was physically able. Yet with the diagnosis of bipolar, Barrett was subject to the vote of his team whether or not he could stay with the Raiders. The stigma keeps its sufferers at arms length, as most people do not understand the disorder, whether it be that of a professional athlete such as Robbins or a teenager like Ryan.

Mr. Robbins never made it back to professional football. I did not hear much about him until two years later. I heard a news report saying Mr. Barret Robbins had been shot in a scuffle with police in Miami, Florida. The following is an article about it.

"Depression, Alcoholism, His Demons"

This was the title of an article from the San Jose Mercury News, January 19, 2005, written by Mark Emmons:

When former Raider Barret Robbins suffered a mental breakdown and went AWOL before the 2003 Super Bowl -- going on a Tijuana drinking binge that left him tearfully talking of suicide -- it seemed his life had hit rock bottom.

Instead, it turns out that Robbins' downward spiral has taken him to even greater, and more tragic, depths.

Robbins, who has battled the twin demons of bipolar disorder and alcoholism, remains in a south Florida hospital in critical but stable condition after being shot at least twice during a violent struggle with police Saturday night. A Miami Beach detective also was knocked unconscious.

As of Tuesday, police had not been able to interview the heavily sedated Robbins. So authorities, who were responding to a burglary call, have no idea why he was in a women's restroom in a South Beach office building. Or why he was even in Miami.

It's yet another bizarre chapter for the troubled former All-Pro center and father of two daughters.

Often people with serious bipolar, especially males, will go from one bizarre experience to another.

Acquaintances of Robbins, 31, have described him as a good -- even gentle -- man caught in the throes of a disease he apparently cannot control. The shooting comes just weeks after Robbins was charged on Christmas Eve for assaulting a San Francisco hotel security guard.

"It's just sad," said Raiders tight end Teyo Johnson. "You talk to anyone who knows Barret really well and they will tell you he's a great guy and a very generous person with a huge heart. Everybody loves Barret. Everybody. He's never mean to anybody."

Yet he also has demonstrated wild mood

swings and the capacity for violence. Mental health experts say such erratic behavior can be seen in extreme cases of bipolar disorder -- a brain chemistry ailment that also is known as manic-depressive illness. It can be treated with medication but is not curable.

"People with this condition just do not have control of their behavior at times," said sports psychologist Richard Lustberg. "If you look at his crimes-against-society behavior, he's starting to look like Mike Tyson, who also suffers from depression. He's heading in a direction that you don't wish for anyone."

I saw this with my son Ryan many times in his life. He exhibited good and even wonderful traits. He was very caring and sensitive. He could tell when you were not doing well and ask what was wrong? He was extremely perceptive about the feelings of others.

This is a sobering story to me as a father of a son with bipolar. I believe it was an inner fear my wife and I had regarding what could happen with Ryan.

He had a volatile temper and acted out aggressive behavior a number of times out in the streets. What would happen if he went too far in a fit of rage while on substance? We constantly prayed Ryan would never injure anyone or get hurt himself.

I am sure we have all heard of various crimes committed by someone who had bipolar. That's part of the ongoing unsettledness a family affected by this disorder lives with.

Searching For Answers
The article continued:

In Robbins' hometown of Houston, Texas, Bobby Plummer doesn't understand what happened to his former star.

"All this stuff has been shock after shock because he's as good a kid as I've ever had," said Plummer, the retired Sharpstown High football coach. "And I'm not just talking about athletes. I'm talking all of them."

Robbins was raised by a single mom and Plummer remembers that Kay Robbins, who died of a sudden illness in 1999, and her son were extremely close. Plummer also recalls Robbins being active in the Fellowship of Christian Athletes and having a soft spot for the school's special education students.

"Some of them were in wheelchairs and others were in real bad shape mentally," Plummer said. "Barret would work with them. They loved him. They called him Big Bear. We'd take the kids by bus to this park in Houston and he wheeled them around, threw balls to them."

A person suffering from bipolar can be as nice a person as you would ever meet, then out of nowhere change into a wild, angry maniac. That is obviously the manic side of the disorder. (4)

It was interesting to see so many similarities between

Barret Robbins and Ryan's story.

What Might Have Been

I often wonder what might have happened with my son had he not taken his life. Here we see a true story about a talented young man plagued with the dual disease of bipolar and substance abuse. It is not a pretty story. Yet it begs the question, how many other people in our society are suffering similar symptoms? How many homeless, alcoholics, drug addicts and criminals find themselves in dire straits because of the disorder of bipolar?

Barret Robbins started out with a good heart. He was a caring person. He was blessed with physical and athletic talent that earned him fame and money. But none of that was able to prepare him to deal with the inner torments of his mind.

I am only one person crying out about how devastating this and other disorders like it are tearing families and individuals apart.

As you will see, a major part of this book emphasizes the need for the awareness of bipolar disorder and the dangers of self-medication with substances which can lead to suicidal thinking. It is my prayer that much more research and funds will be raised and dedicated to the study of medical cures for bipolar disorder, ADHD, depression, substance abuse and suicide.

Kenneth Dignan

Chapter Two

Spinning Out of Control

When our son was sixteen years old he told us that he was experimenting with drugs and alcohol. We were disappointed, but relieved at his honesty. We realized illegal substances are plentiful and easily available to most high school students.

We suspected it, especially when he acted rebellious and angry. He constantly disobeyed us. We did all the usual responsible parent things: grounding him, taking away his allowance, car privileges, checking his breath when he came home late at night, all to no avail. He appeared to be spinning out of control, exhibiting extreme mood swings and fits of rage. We just thought that he was going through that rebellious teen-age phase, but were unaware of the hell that was going on inside his mind.

Self-Medicating

Our son told us he felt better immediately after drinking alcohol or smoking marijuana. This is the crux of the matter that centers on the instant gratification of substances. While prescription medications can provide some relief, they usually take 3 to 5 weeks, and sometimes longer, to make a difference and or be felt.

One can feel alcohol or drugs immediately. That is why a

number of people with bipolar also have a dual diagnosis of substance abuse. The two often go hand in hand.

Those with bipolar are desperately looking for something that will stop their racing thoughts, their anxiety, their feelings of boredom which can lead to anger. While medications are the long term answer, along with therapy, substance is the quick fix. It is easier to do substances with your friends than to tell them, "I can't drink because I'm on medication." Substances fit right in with the "party scene."

Though drugs are illegal, teenagers and adults alike still take them at a party and are able to get up for school and or work the next day. Those with bipolar disorder often cannot function well the next day due to a serious chemical imbalance.

No Easy Answers

Ryan would often say, "Why can my friends drink and smoke pot and not go crazy or loose their temper after substance? They can act normal the next day and do what they have too. But I can't?" Usually the one with bipolar does not grasp or want to accept the bi-product of self-medication.

I believe overcoming substance abuse can happen in a miraculous way through prayer and faith in God. One can receive wonderful help through various programs such as, Teen Challenge and Alcoholics Anonymous.

However, through much research, I have learned that numerous individuals who have mood disorders experience a greater difficulty recovering from their addictions. Many become chronic substance abusers, going from rehab to rehab.

In my endless search for answers, I even wondered if certain street drugs, such as Ecstasy, could have caused Ryan's bipolar. However, one of Ryan's doctors felt strongly that our son was genetically predisposed to the disorder, meaning that he would have manifested the symptoms at some time and probably did even as a child. Whatever the origination of the dreaded diagnosis, Ryan was indeed in trouble.

Something Was Different

When Ryan was a junior in high school, he was excited about the challenges before him. Because of his high grade point average, he was invited to take advanced placement courses to prepare him for testing to receive college credit.

After completing summer camp for varsity football, Ryan felt pretty good. He worked hard trying to secure playing time as a tight end. With his boundless energy he would go to those long, hot, high school summer football camps.

I was amazed how he did all the drills, ran endless laps around the track, lifted weights and did his best to prepare for the fall season. I sometimes drove over to the football field to watch the workouts. It would take me a few minutes before I spotted my son, but eventually I located him and studied his every move. He was so much fun to watch. When I picked him up after the workouts he never complained, never said he wanted to quit or that he could not handle it. I believed he had what it took to become a good high school football player and possibly to play in college.

A Football Setback

It was customary for a senior football player to gain the starting position for a game. Often the juniors would be benchwarmers and role players. In Ryan's case he spent more time on the bench than he cared to. His coach still believed in him and often found a way for him to get in for a few plays to gain experience for the next year because he was being groomed to be the starter.

During the game against Homewood Flossmoor High School he got to see a lot of playing time. It was a very cold and windy evening. Ryan made some tremendous plays and I saw some light at the end of the tunnel. Maybe he was getting better at accepting his role.

Something Was Still Going Wrong

Along with this athletic hurdle, Ryan felt pressure in the advanced placement classes. The work level was more difficult and required more time for homework and projects, than he was willing to give. Instead he chose the constant interaction with friends and going out every night, his very own prescription for dealing with his own inner turmoil.

His grades began to slip and he started causing disruptions in the classroom, often losing his temper. Occasionally a teacher would get word to us that they saw something different in Ryan's behavior.

He was acting more rebellious and hard to control at home as he continued partying with drugs and alcohol. Though we kept telling him it was not healthy, he still went out with his friends every night. Surrounded by friends, at the end of the first semester of his junior year, Ryan remained upset and no better.

Most of the time we lived as the old cliché so aptly describes, "On pins and needles." We never knew when Ryan would come home in a rage because of something that had gone wrong with his friends. We nervously anticipated his return home in the wee hours of the night. Would he be drunk, would he be coming down from a night of ecstasy, or another mind-destroying drug?

But it wasn't limited to just the effects of drugs or alcohol. Bipolar caused Ryan to have racing thoughts that wouldn't let him sleep, and he'd stay up all night playing music or driving his car around for hours. We waited up as we couldn't sleep either, worrying about our son.

The Dreaded Holidays

Instead of anticipating holidays, we came to dread them. "What catastrophe would occur this time?" This was always in the back of our mind.

I remember one Thanksgiving when two of Joni's sisters and their families were visiting from Minnesota. Ryan refused to come out of his room for dinner. Joni went up to talk to him and he erupted into a rage. Nothing could stop him or calm him down when he was in a manic mood. His cousins looked on in amazement as Ryan shoved his mother out of his room yelling at her at the top of his lungs. Believe me it was very hard to be thankful that holiday.

I later came to believe the holidays were extremely depressing and painful for Ryan, as they were suppose to be times when everyone is happy and celebrating while he only felt a heavy cloud of depression and unwelcome thoughts.

We learned to live almost as recluses, never knowing what to expect from Ryan. We often chose instead to avoid entertaining during those days.

It was difficult to have a normal family life as we walked on eggshells not wanting to cause Ryan to explode in a fit of anger. Seeing Ryan act in these times prior to the official diagnosis of bipolar was extremely hard.

Trying to Salvage Junior Year

When Ryan went back to school following Christmas break, we noticed he was very hesitant and tentative. Every morning it was a huge task just getting him out of bed. He barely made it to school and usually tardy.

He blamed teachers for not being fair with him in expectations of some assignments. He would come home after school and tell me he was getting into sharp disagreements with his classmates and wanting to fight them. This kind of behavior was a sign to us he was not doing well.

Then we heard something I thought I would never hear from Ryan. Our honor roll student and our great athlete said, "I'm dropping out of school." How could that be? We found out he did not sign up for spring wrestling, which he loved his freshman and sophomore years. This was not the same person we knew and loved. We made him go to school as much as we could, but eventually he totally closed down and refused to go to classes.

We explained to the school authorities that our son was

having some type of emotional problem. We took him to our doctor and he diagnosed Ryan as suffering from depression and anxiety. He prescribed some medication and recommended therapy with a counselor. This was prior to the official diagnosis of bipolar

From February to May of 2000, we arranged for tutors from his high school to come to the house for Ryan. It was a struggle to get him to study and be ready when the tutors came. He almost totally withdrew from his friends, experiencing extreme paranoia.

By the grace of God and much effort and encouragement from homebound teachers, and us, he passed his classes and got credit for his junior year. We optimistically thought he might be able to get back into the swing of things the next year. Instead it was one problem after another. This scenario is repeated time and again in the life of an individual with serious bipolar disorder and substance abuse.

Various Descriptions of Bipolar Feelings

Descriptions offered by people with bipolar disorder give valuable insights into the various mood states associated with the illness:

<u>Depression</u>: I doubt completely my ability to do anything well. It seems as though my mind has slowed down and burned out to the point of being virtually useless.... [I am] haunt[ed]... with the total, the desperate hopelessness of it all.... Others say, "It's only temporary, it will pass, you will get over it," but of course they haven't any idea of how I feel, although they are certain they do. If I can't feel, move, think or care, then what on earth is the point?

<u>Hypomania</u>: At first when I'm high, it's tremendous… ideas are fast… like shooting stars you follow until brighter ones appear…. All shyness disappears, the right words and gestures are suddenly there, uninteresting people, things, become intensely interesting. Your marrow is infused with unbelievable feelings of ease, power, well-being, omnipotence, euphoria…you can do anything…but, somewhere this changes.

<u>Mania</u>: The fast ideas become too fast and there are far too many… overwhelming confusion replaces clarity… you stop keeping up with it—memory goes. Infectious humor ceases to amuse. Your friends become frightened…. everything is now against the grain… you are irritable, angry, frightened, uncontrollable, and trapped. (1)

Fond Memories

Though this book zeros in on a painful four-year period of Ryan's life, we have numerous wonderful and fond memories of his childhood. He was our bundle of energy, our adventurer, explorer and student. In his earlier grades we never had to tell him to do his homework or get good grades. He would go straight home from school and do his homework, not going outside to play until it was completely done.

He loved going to the Indiana Dunes with his closest friends, Jack, Tommy and Jimmy. He ran around those sand dunes and jumped in and out of the lake all day. Sleepovers were a blast because Ryan could be very funny and act like a clown. He loved to entertain his friends. We heard them making racket all night till dawn.

We have beloved pictures of his friends in GI Joe camouflage paint as they played night tag on a birthday sleepover.

He belonged to a church club for teenage boys called the "Royal Rangers." He tirelessly worked to earn badges for memorizing scriptures, to knife throwing, chopping wood, setting up camp and building a fire.

He was a self-starter and highly motivated to be the best at whatever he did, sometimes to a fault. Looking back this may have been a precursor that something was wrong.

Kenneth Dignan

Chapter Three

The Hospital Merry-Go-Round

The chronicle of Ryan's experiences that he had in hospitals and rehab centers from January 3, 2000 to July 21, 2002, will illustrate the length a family will go, to seek healing for a child who has an emotional illness. So far I've shared various random thoughts of our experiences with Ryan. But the next two chapters will give an in-depth and orderly breakdown of what went on with the medical community and Ryan.

The heartbreaking downward progression of a teenager who was never sick or hospitalized to one, who ended up in and out of numerous hospitals and rehabs, seeking a cure, still brings a painful jab to my heart whenever I think about it.

Christ Hospital, Oak Lawn, Illinois, January 3, 2000

Ryan was acting extremely hyper, pacing and wild-eyed. We suspected he was high on some substance so we forced him to go to the emergency room. When I say by force, I mean we had to call the paramedics to come and get Ryan. When they came, he refused to cooperate with them so they strapped him to a gurney and put him in the ambulance. This was typical of all the times we suggested he get help. He never went willingly.

The emergency room was filled to capacity with flu

victims, so Ryan was kept in the hallway for a long time. He desperately wanted to leave. They finally got him into a room and only the threat of cauterization convinced him to give the nurses a urine sample for a drug test. Or might I say, all the doctors and nurses stood on their heads to get him to cooperate.

That night Joni and I tried to get Ryan admitted to the hospital for observation. While we were working with the staff in admissions, knowing our sons desire to leave, we asked some security guards to keep their eyes on him. But it was too late, Ryan escaped out the door. The hospital called the police; they came, got a description and arranged an area search. We were, of course, frantic as we imagined a distraught and desperate teenager loose on the streets of the Chicago area.

While on the run, Ryan called his brother Patrick from a nearby bowling alley and asked him to come and get him. When we arrived home we were shocked to find out he was already there.

We had tried all night to get our son help and here we were again, empty handed, trying to figure out what to do next.

Palos Primary Care, Orland Park, Illinois, June 2000

That summer he continued to go out almost every night. He was extremely hard for us to control. If we tried to make him stay home, he would go out anyway. He often got very angry if we told him do anything he did not want to. Someone with bipolar has frequent moods of irritability and anger. They have an extreme need to get their own way no matter what the cost. There can be threats of doing themselves harm or breaking something in the house. When Ryan wasn't getting his way he would punch a hole in the drywall or pick up a plate or coaster and throw it. Our home often became a war zone as Ryan released his rage.

In June of 2000, Ryan was sitting with some neighborhood friends on their driveway. I went over and asked him to come home. It sent him into a wild rage. He ran to my van and did a high karate kick and dented the back passenger side. He then jumped on to the hood of his mother's car and put a huge dent in that. He kicked in the basement window and began throwing things around the house. The whole neighborhood looked on as he freaked out. His friends tried to calm him down, but he ran into the backyard and jumped over the fence injuring his knee. His friends tried to hold him to the ground, but he broke free.

He left with his girlfriend and we did not see him all night. Our hearts were broken, as we alternately worried and felt relieved that he was gone and the havoc was over for the time being. The next day we discovered that his girl-friend's mother, concerned about his leg, took him to an Immediate Care Center. He came home in a leg brace having sprained his knee.

Ryan would come home often after such episodes, offer no apology and act as though he did nothing wrong. In fact he was good at twisting circumstances, pointing fingers and somehow making it our fault. We were left with a broken heart, broken house, broken dreams and yet he couldn't understand why we were upset.

From Palos Hospital to Riveredge Hospital
Forest Park, Illinois, July 21, 2000

This was the point of no return that opened this book. Ryan had crashed his mother's car into a children's park around 11:00 pm. The police sent Ryan to Palos Hospital in Palos Heights, Illinois. Not equipped to deal with a patient like our son, the Palos Hospital secured a bed for Ryan at a lockdown rehab center called Riveredge in Forest Park, Illinois. This facility diagnosed and treated troubled young people with psychological and substance problems.

I drove there with my father, Joni following in her car, and we arrived at the same time the ambulance did. As Ryan was sitting on the gurney, looking dazed and confused, my father had tears in his eyes to see his grandchild in this situation. Yet we hoped he was in a place where finally we could get to the bottom of what was going on with our son. They gave him numerous tests, group therapy and sessions with a psychiatrist, social worker and a therapist.

It hurt to see how far he had fallen. Everywhere at Riveredge were similar kids in similar situations. I thought Ryan should not be in here. He was a normal kid from a normal home.

Ryan called several times a day begging us to get him out. He was afraid of losing his girlfriend and all of his friends. He worried people would think he was crazy.

The hospital gave him medication to calm him down. The specialists assured us they would do their best to determine how to help our son. After many tests and evaluations, the doctors diagnosed him with bipolar disorder or manic-depression. He was there for several days.

Specialists usually look at a number of aspects for a diagnosis. In "Schizophrenia and Bipolar Disorders a Family Manual," Dr Herbert Wagemaker says "1. Presenting Symptoms; thinking, mood, affect, behavior and perception. 2. Natural History; ages that the patient exhibited certain symptoms and their frequency of occurrence. 3. Family History; were there any family members who suffer from mental illness or substance abuse? Sometimes this relative is an aunt, uncle, or a grandparent who died in the state hospital. I look for depression, alcoholism, or bipolar disorder these point to a history of affective or mood disorders in the family." (1)

We were told he had all the classic symptoms including hyperactivity, manic episodes of racing thoughts, anger and rage to bouts with depression and hopelessness. The doctors also said he had a dual diagnosis of substance abuse.

Bipolar Defined

Dr. Wagemaker goes on to say, "Bipolar is a brain disease. It has to do with brain chemistry that is askew or broken. The brain chemistry has problems adjusting to moods and fluctuates between two poles, thus the term bipolar."

"Extended periods of hopelessness, pessimism and fear create an intense feeling that life is not worth living. These feelings can become so intense that the bipolar individual often becomes addicted to alcohol or drugs."

Doctor Wagemaker says that some people in a manic stage experience racing thoughts. It is as if their minds are exploding. "They cannot contain all their thoughts. In a depressed cycle the thought process seems slower; they procrastinate and cannot make decisions. Often they feel people are against them and the world is also against them (paranoia). Life in general is overwhelming. They feel hopeless and helpless. They even have suicidal thoughts. During this time, twenty-five percent of patients (not following treatment) commit suicide." (2)

We saw these symptoms overtake our son and hold him captive. I experienced great emotional pain to see my son suffer. He was being held hostage by a chemical imbalance in his own brain.

Rush Mental Health Center in Palos Heights, Illinois

After he was released from Riveredge, he attended an outpatient substance abuse program for around two months.

Though I had heard of clinical depression and chemical imbalance in the brain, I was not prepared for the nightmare a mental disorder can cause. I believed anyone could overcome depression if they faced it head on and battled through, with God's help, to make something positive out of a bad situation

Why couldn't Ryan tough it out? Why wouldn't he just take his medicine, stop doing substances, follow the doctor's orders, and do whatever it took to live successfully with this thing? Why couldn't he look at it as a challenge to overcome like he used to with his classes and athletic endeavors? Something was now very different and it was only getting worse.

Dual Diagnosis

At the 1996 U.S. Psychiatric and Mental Health

Congress, Kathleen Brady. M.D., Ph.D., an associate professor of Psychiatry at the Medical University of South Carolina, reported that substance abuse occurs in thirty percent to sixty percent of patients with bipolar disorder and is more likely to co-exist with bipolar illness than with any other Axis I psychiatric disorder.

In The Dual Diagnosis: Adolescents with Co-occurring Brain Disorders and Substance Abuse Disorders, Brenda Souto offers that the combination of mental illness and substance abuse is so common that many clinicians now expect to find it. The term self-medication, then, is defined as the process by which some individuals may abuse substances in an attempt to use them to relieve other problems such as anxiety, pain, sleeplessness or other symptoms of bipolar disorder. (3)

Nick Traina

In reading the story of Nick Traina, "His Bright Light," I saw striking similarities with Ryan. He was a handsome, outgoing and smart young boy when he was drawn to substance. He suffered from manic-depression and committed suicide at 19 years of age.

His mother, famous author Danielle Steel writes,

"Things began to go seriously wrong for Nick that year (seventh grade). He began to experiment with drugs. Others have tried it at the same age, and come out the other end, but like everything else Nick did, Nick fell into it with a certain manic passion. He drank a little and tried pot, and along

with a group of friends, late in the school year, he tried acid (LSD)."

Nick struggled on and off with being able to stay in school so his mother put him in a boarding school. One day the school said, "Something was seriously wrong with Nick, and that leaving him there was an invitation to disaster. He's not capable of being here, they said. He needs treatment. He couldn't follow the rules, not so much didn't, as couldn't...They felt that something was off about him, they had noticed his lack of impulse control, and the crazy things he did...It was obvious that Nick was no longer able to function in an ordinary environment. He couldn't play by the rules anymore. He was slowly losing the ability to control himself." (4)

No Laughing Matter

An individual with a mood disorder or brain disease such as bipolar, schizophrenia, psychosis or paranoia is often bright and creative. But an abnormality in their brain chemistry causes them to think and act abnormally.

They might appear uncooperative and combative but that's the way their brain chemistry imbalance causes them to act. The goal of medicine and psychiatry is to find medications that can correct the chemical imbalance. However, for some, such as Ryan, all the medications in the world may not alleviate the symptoms of this disorder because they continue doing substances. It is a medical fact that alcohol or drugs used during treatment counteract any benefit the medications might provide.

Medications Can Alter "Feeling Normal"

Often, the "Ryan's" of this disorder do not believe they need to keep taking medications. When feeling better while on substance, they think everything is fine. Then when not taking substances, they feel rejected, alone, and unable to establish meaningful relationships. The chemical imbalance in Ryan's brain that caused his mood swings and depression sidelined him. No longer could he participate in the things he loved without extreme duress.

Ryan hated not being able to feel like his old self. He did not like the way the medications made him feel. Depakote, a drug used for seizures, is often used to treat bipolar disorder. This medication made Ryan gain weight and this self-conscious kid hated getting "fat." He would stop taking many of the medications prescribed by the doctors claiming they made him feel lethargic and numb.

He did not like the side effects most medications used to treat bipolar disorder caused. He rather believed he felt better by using certain street drugs and alcohol even though it only provided temporary relief and did more damage than good.

Standard Counseling May Not Always Help

In my years as a pastoral counselor and minister, there have been countless hurting souls who poured out their hearts to me. I have spent hours in counseling sessions with troubled people and most were just looking for someone to listen to them share their pain and frustrations. I would give them some advice, share some relevant scripture passages and encourage a different pattern of behavior. In some cases they followed my advice and were able to handle their difficulties better.

I tried the same approach with Ryan but could tell it would not be that simple. When my son confronted his own mental battlefield, I prayed he would be able to side step the many landmines that were apparent.

Hopes of a New High School

The staff at Riveredge Hospital suggested that he make new friends, who were not involved in substance abuse. With his disorder it was essential he abstain from any alcohol or drugs.

We enrolled him as a senior at a private high school close to our home. We believed he would find new friends with a Christian background. Ryan frequently told his mother that he prayed all the time and realized he needed the Lord's help and that a new beginning would be good for him.

We experienced a glimmer of hope as Ryan began his senior year at Chicago Christian High School in Palos Heights, Illinois. He made new friends, and even met a wonderful girl he took on a few dates.

Still Ryan could not concentrate on his classes. He was caught smoking outside the school. He got into personality conflicts with other students. School administrators were very concerned about Ryan's problems. He lasted there only two months. Again our hope was short lived. It was evident to me that we would need all the help and faith we could muster up to survive this nightmare.

Now What?

Out of school at the age of eighteen, Ryan had too much time on his hands. We encouraged him to get a job so that it would at least fill a void. He finally found temporary work for the Christmas holidays at a sporting goods store.

He did pretty well at the job and why not? Ryan was an outgoing, easy-to-like person and we hoped he could stick it out. Yet he did not last. He missed work often, unable to get out of bed due to depression. He thought his bosses did not like him, and paranoia crept in as he was extra sensitive and imagined they were purposely trying to make it hard for him. This resulted in him getting fired before Christmas, another tough holiday for Ryan and our family.

Kenneth Dignan

Chapter Four

The Hospital Merry-Go-Round Continues

This not so merry-go-round of hospitals, treatments and trials continued with no end in sight.

Talking about G.E.D.

After the holidays of 2000, my brothers hired Ryan to work at their construction site. He worked there for a number of months and we did our best to get him to take his medications and see his doctor and his counselors, so he could stay on an even keel.

Feeling more hopeful he began to talk about taking the GED exam and getting his high school diploma. He wanted to attend Western Illinois University where his brother, Patrick, was a junior.

Ryan ordered the forms and sent them in so he could be assigned a date to take the GED exams. The date came back and off he went, confident he'd do well.

A few weeks later he received the reports and he passed everything with above-average scores. This showed me how brilliant he really was. It broke my heart to imagine what a young man with such a tremendous aptitude for learning could have achieved had not bipolar ensnared him.

The past year and a half had been difficult for him, but he finally had his high school diploma. We helped him fill out his application and financial aid forms. He sent them in and eventually was accepted at Western. His mother borrowed a truck; they packed it to capacity with his belongings and she drove him to college. He started Western Illinois University in August, 2001. Could this be the beginning of things turning around for Ryan? He was cautiously optimistic, yet excited about entering college life. "Hope against hope," was our motto, and the reality of our existence.

McDonough County Hospital, Macomb, Illinois, October 20, 2001

Ryan really hoped he would feel halfway normal while attending Western. We were worried whether he would actually be able to attend classes, remember to take his medications and do his homework.

We called him often and he always said everything was OK. I wanted to go to the campus and check up on him periodically, but we lived four hours away. I opted for the trust and hope factor.

But on Saturday morning, October 20, 2001, the McDonough County Hospital called and said our son was there. Apparently Ryan had barricaded himself in his dorm room the night before and threatened to kill himself. The authorities broke in and sent him to the hospital by ambulance. He had not been taking his medications and was using substances again.

Later, we found out that he only attended his classes

sporadically. He had been sucked into the college party scene and rarely attended his classes. His illness and addictions dragged him into deeper despair.

Apart from his illness he was a fun-loving, caring person who often sensed when a family member or friend was going through something. He tried to lift people's spirits even though he fought his own darkness. He was trapped by a mind that would not let him go. Bipolar was stealing his life.

My oldest son, Andy, volunteered to go to Macomb, Illinois, with his wife Jodi, to pick up his brother and bring him home. Andy and Jodi became extremely close to Ryan, and he would reach out to them many times to help him. As the older brother, Andy felt a deep responsibility toward him.

When Ryan returned home we tried to get his body chemistry balanced out. We endeavored to get him back on his medication, and he did well for a while. As usual his disorder made him too stubborn to do what was best for him.

We told him if he wanted to live at home he had to cooperate. We realized he was in no shape to work at a regular job. A boss who would cut him some slack and make allowances for days when his depression locked him captive to his bed would be hard to find. So I hired him to work for me part-time as a driver and office manager.

He tried to abstain from hanging out with his old friends, but soon gave in as the loneliness of isolation overcame him. The vicious circle of substance abuse, fierce emotions, and destructive behavior began. We asked him to leave our home a number of times, but he always begged to come back. One evening, late at night, he began pounding on the doors and windows until we let him in. The counselors shouted "Co-dependence!" We yelled back, "Survival!"

Eventually we came to realize the difficulty for someone with such severe bipolar to respond successfully to behavioral modification or standard disciplinary rules. It was easier to tell him to leave the house if he didn't obey the rules. One of Ryan's doctors said to us, "Would you kick your son out if he had diabetes or cancer?" Of course we could not. Thus, we stretched the limits of our patience, understanding and love as we continued to help our son face the disorder of bipolar.

For the next six months Ryan worked for me as my driver and assisted me with errands for the church and Til Healing Comes Ministries.

Rock Creek Treatment Center, Lemont, Illinois
April 30-May 10, 2002 (Closed in 2003)

On April 29, 2002, Joni and I went to Tinley Park Mental Health group for guidance from a psychiatrist. We were not sure what to do next, but it was evident Ryan needed to be placed somewhere fast.

On April 30th, early in the morning, I took steps to go before a judge and convince him that Ryan was a danger to himself and others. Once a week, a judge held court at the Tinley Park mental health center for people seeking to gain help from the legal authorities. I went before him and was granted a court order to become his temporary legal guardian so I could place him in another rehab center.

We decided to bring Ryan to the Rock Creek Center in

Lemont, Illinois. We developed a plan to get an independent ambulance company and the Cook County Sheriff to assist us in picking Ryan up at our home as he slept. Knowing Ryan would not go willingly, I believed the surprise approach would be more successful. When they arrived he resisted but was subdued and sent to the center by an ambulance.

Once again the doctors and staff offered us hope and the possibility that Ryan had a chance at living a normal life.

Ryan was very angry that we put him in another rehab center. He accused us of putting him in there because we hated him. He just could not see that we did it because we wanted him to get well.

The scenario became similar to our other experiences. Ryan had good days and bad days. Sometimes he would understand the importance of participating in the group and individual therapy sessions. He would take his medications and accept he had to be there.

At other times he became upset at the whole situation and threatened to leave. He would call us and beg to be discharged. He promised to listen to us, to take his medications, to stay off substance, get a job and come home on time. We heard it all before.

Safe Haven Halfway Housing, Alsip, Illinois
May 10-17, 2002

After eight days at the Rock Creek Center the doctors and therapists believed Ryan was well enough to be released. We felt he was not ready to leave, but they said due to insurance policies and the usual length of stay, he had to be discharged. They suggested he go to a place called Safe Haven Halfway House for a more extended follow up.

Ryan reluctantly agreed when we told him he could not come home until he had a more stable life. He lived in an apartment complex with others who had psychological disorders and abused substances. He had to attend Alcoholics Anonymous meetings daily. He could work at a job during the day and come and go as he pleased. There was a strict nighttime schedule of an eleven o'clock curfew.

During this time my youngest brother, Marty, hired Ryan to assist him with breaking down a concrete patio. He picked Ryan up every morning at the halfway house and drove him to work. At the conclusion of that job, my brother found Ryan a position at a millwork company.

At first, Marty picked Ryan up and took him to the millwork, but after a couple of weeks Ryan refused to keep living at the Safe Haven Halfway House and wanted to come home. We felt it was not a good idea. What would have been accomplished after all this if he ended up back at home again so soon?

The only thing we could come up with was to have him move in with his grandparents. They agreed and hoped he would follow a few basic rules, like come home right after work, eat dinner with them, and come in at night by 11:00 p.m. We agreed to let him use our old car to drive to work if he kept his job and stayed at grandma and grandpas.

That arrangement only lasted a few days. Ryan stayed out late at night and did not come home for dinner. My parents could not handle it at their age. He had to leave their home and come back to ours.

A few weeks later he quit the job. He was convinced some people that worked there did not like him. This was a pattern of paranoid behavior we were all too familiar with.

True to his inability to think and access situations clearly, he could not hold a job. From all my reading on the subject, this behavior is all too familiar with victims of bipolar disorder.

Palos Hospital, Palos Heights, Illinois, June 9, 2002

On Saturday, June 8, 2002, Ryan came in around 1:00 a.m. after a friend brought him home. Our oldest son, Andy, was home visiting, and heard a car door shut and then heard Ryan yelling that some guys were after him. Andy went out and saw his brother running down the street kicking parked cars. Andy got Ryan back into the house and called 911. An ambulance took Ryan to the local hospital again, where they said Ryan admitted to drinking a whole bottle of gin.

Riveredge Hospital, Forest Park, Illinois
June 9-17, 2002

Ryan was transferred back to Riveredge Hospital. He had numerous sessions with a psychiatrist, a therapist, and group therapy. For eight days he was back in the treatment center promising to do better.

Ryan agreed to sign a family contract to stay on his medications, go to Alcoholics Anonymous, and stay away from his friends who used substances. He was released but only a few days later Ryan broke that contract again, and he went back on substances.

Palos Hospital, Palos Heights, Illinois, June 20, 2002

On June 19, 2002 two of Ryan's friends were killed while driving their motorcycles. He and his other friends spent the night at the accident site setting up a memorial. Early the next morning Ryan came home and began talking to his mother. He seemed hyper and very talkative.

He started speaking about the Book of Revelation, about the end times and terrorism. He was concerned about the spiritual condition of his friends who were killed in the accident. He said he was talking to his other friends about Jesus and the Bible.

After an hour of talking to his mother, he came up to my bedroom to talk to me about God and the Bible. He was genuinely concerned about others and showed an honest interest in spiritual things.

He wanted to be sure all his friends were told about how to get to heaven. He also talked about bizarre things like the possibility and fear of terrorists trying to attack the Sears Tower. I grew concerned about his intensity and anxiousness. I noticed his hands were purple and red spots appeared on his face and arms.

Seeing his physical appearance and noticing his inability to talk logically I knew I had to call an ambulance to take Ryan back to the hospital. I made numerous calls to the hospital, our insurance company, the police and the fire department and set up the plan to get Ryan, by force, to the hospital.

When the ambulance arrived, Ryan ran out of the

house in his T-shirt, jeans and socks. The police tracked him down a few blocks away and put him into the ambulance.

He continued talking about the end times while he was in the emergency room at Palos Hospital. Joni kept asking him if he had done any drugs. He denied any such thing.

The nurses took urine and blood, which was now a regular occurrence. Ryan had talked non-stop to anyone who came into his room. We found out the tests revealed he had cocaine and marijuana in his system. It was just two days after getting out of Riveredge treatment center.

Riveredge Hospital, Forest Park, Illinois
June 20-25, 2002

We transferred Ryan back to Riveredge, straight from Palos Hospital. He stayed there for two or three days and became more stabilized. The relief that came, once he was separated from his friends and substance, was tangible. Considering, we were finally able to have a peaceful sleep.

Calvary Center New Life Clinic, Phoenix, Arizona
June 25-July 21, 2002

Knowing our son needed more intensive therapy, I prayed to find a place to send Ryan. I was led to look into the New Life Clinic, a part of the Minerth-Mier Christian counseling program. They had a twenty-eight day therapy program in Phoenix, Arizona, Calvary Center. Ryan was now nineteen years old and had been in and out of numerous hospitals and rehab programs. We never gave up hope that one would work. He was our son. His mother and

I vowed to do whatever it took to help him find peace and purpose in life.

We told him he needed to get away from our town and its influences. He eventually agreed. So, on June 25 my wife picked Ryan up at Riveredge Hospital and took him to Midway airport for his first airline flight, bound for Phoenix.

Once there Ryan called us after only a few days and wanted to leave. We told him he could not come home. We had paid a non-refundable fee of $6500 up front. He said he would try to get with the program. He called us almost two times a day. He told me he felt uncomfortable there and did not feel it was for him.

During the 4th of July holiday, we got a phone call saying Ryan was upset and disturbed. He wanted to leave the program. The staff person wanted to call the police to take him to the station. The next step would be to kick him out of the program and he would be out on the streets over a thousand miles away. The center had a smaller staff for the holiday. It was obvious this staff member didn't know how to deal with a person suffering from bipolar.

I pleaded with them to call the psychiatrist who was working with our son there and get his advice instead of calling the police. They did and Ryan was taken to the hospital to check his medication levels. The doctor started him on a medication called lithobid, a derivative of lithium, which has been used to treat manic-depression (bipolar) for many years.

After a few days, he was returned to the center. He settled down and began to work with the program. Whether it was the new medicine or the realization we weren't going to let him come home until he finished the program or a combination of factors. He was able to find a good therapist he felt comfortable with who understood him. Twenty-eight days later he was able to graduate. Joni attended his graduation ceremony in Phoenix and brought him back home the next day.

At home, he seemed much better, calmer and centered. He allowed me to read Scripture with him and study the Bible. He seemed like he had more hope and resolve to fight through all his pain and darkness. Were we out of the woods? Was Ryan on the road to recovery? We sure desired the best for him and prayed he was on his way to recovery and a chance for a better life.

It was amazing how clear headed he acted. We saw openness to God and discussions about the Bible and faith. He had gone 28 days with no drugs or alcohol in his system. What a difference it made. I hoped and prayed earnestly he could stay clean and sober. I held my breath everyday that went by when he did not call an old friend or say he wanted to go out with them. How long could this last?

It proved to me that a dual diagnosis of bipolar and substance abuse was definitely a double-edged sword. Removing the substance made it more possible to deal with the bipolar. Sure he still had times of depression, manic episodes, irritability and the like. But as he kept on his medication and stayed away from all the wrong influences he had a chance to survive.

We saw something we had not seen in a long time, our old son Ryan. When he was clean from any substance his true kind, caring and loving self would come out. Deep inside there was an awesome young man, a son that would make any parent proud.

I prayed, "if only Ryan would be able to never touch another drop of alcohol or take another mind altering substance and take his medication along with therapy, he'd be alright."

Chapter Five

Those Dreaded Words

When Ryan got back from the twenty-eight day therapy center in Phoenix, called New Life Clinic, at the end of July 2002, I realized he needed a job. I hired him to work for me again.

Knowing it was a struggle for him to get up; I would call downstairs to his bedroom in the morning between 9:00 a.m. and 9:30 a.m. to see if he felt able to come to work. Sometimes he would say, "OK" and other times he'd say, "I can't, not today". If I really needed him, I would plead, "Ryan, I need your help today. I know how much you want the money". Sometimes it worked, and sometimes it did not.

We became very close and I was happy to have him around driving me and assisting me with office duties. My son showed signs of getting his life back on track, but there were still times of disappointment, both for Ryan and us, his family.

Holding on to Every Minute

Knowing how volatile the situation could get with a child who was bipolar, I tried to hold on to every minute I had with my son. There were days that drained me. At times I envied my wife, who could go to her job at the local high school and get a breather. But she often reminded me he was on her heart every minute of the day.

I was the dad, the protector, and the guardian of my troubled son. I took my calling seriously. It was a blessing that I had the kind of occupation where I could occasionally be flexible with my hours, so I could change my schedule to be available for my son.

Proud to Work for Me

I believed working for me was the best solution for Ryan to have a flexible job and earn a little money. He drove me to my church office, to my brother's construction office, where I worked part time in sales and to the Total Living Network studios, where I recorded my television programs. He also went with me to churches occasionally on Sunday mornings as I spoke, sang, and promoted my book, "Til Healing Comes."

Ryan enjoyed working at the book table where I displayed my book, a gospel music tape I recorded, and various videos. He would listen to me speak and I could tell he soaked in a lot of spiritual truths. I prayed that working for me would help Ryan become stabilized and happy. He could be comfortable knowing I understood his moods and gave him the necessary slack. It also allowed him to earn his own spending money.

Embarrassed About Bipolar

As the months went by I observed that he continued struggling. He often felt embarrassed about having bipolar and the fact that he could not stay in college. One day a minister friend of mine began talking about his son's college accomplishments, and he asked Ryan, "How are you doing in college? What is your major?"

My son looked at me as if to say, "What should I say? Help me Dad." "He tried college, but found it was not for him," I said, "He went to work for me and he loves it." Ryan looked at me with a sigh of relief.

Other's who knew of our son's problems would say, "Isn't he better yet?"

People often asked, "What's wrong with your son? Why isn't he getting better? Why isn't he following the doctor's orders? I thought he'd be over this by now."

The average person who has not experienced this nightmare does not realize that the emotions of everyone involved go up and down constantly. The hope of finding a new therapy, a new medication, a new doctor or therapist is often dashed to the ground as the situation gets no better and sometimes even worse.

After all the hospital stays, doctors, medications, and therapists, our son still struggled greatly. He could not stay faithful to going to Alcoholics Anonymous meetings. It was hard to find one that had some younger men in it. He felt uncomfortable being in AA as he said, "with a bunch of old people who wondered why a 20-year-old kid was there."

Began to Give Up
He began to get bored and lonely so he went back out with his old friends. He started skipping his medicine saying it didn't allow him to feel right. We were afraid he was falling back to his old ways. If he went back to substance it could undo any good he got at New Life Center.

At this time it was very hard to have any hope he would ever be able to cope with bipolar. I will never forget the great pain and agony I felt as a father who longed for his son to feel better and be able to cope with life.

The Christmas holidays were approaching and they were especially difficult for Ryan.

A Puzzling Psychiatric Decision

At the next scheduled doctor's appointment, Ryan told the psychiatrist he wanted to quit taking lithobid because of the way it made him feel, numb to feelings, quiet and withdrawn. The psychiatrist, knowing Ryan's stubbornness, realized it would be a battle to get him to continue taking it, so he said, "Alright, you are the boss, but let's increase the dose of Geodon to compensate."

That frightened my wife and me because we were under the impression that lithium was very important for someone with bipolar and suicidal tendencies, even if he only took it occasionally. When he took it, he had fewer rages and seemed calmer. However he said it made him feel he was not himself, thus skipping doses.

Friday the 13th

On Friday, December 13, 2002, I sent a fax to his doctor encouraging him to tell Ryan to go back on his lithobid. Ryan had stopped taking it altogether, and it appeared he was getting worse. At least when the doctor told us he had to take this medication it gave us enough leverage to hound him to take it even if not all the prescribed doses.

A Busy Day at the Office

At the start of the day, I woke Ryan up around 9:30 a.m. to go to work with me. My television program was giving a special illustrated painting called, "Your Heart in God's Hands," to anyone who made a contribution of fifty dollars or more, to raise funds for airtime costs.

I had ordered a number of fifteen-inch cardboard cylinders to send out the paintings. Ryan was to stuff a Christmas letter and the print into each tube. He also put on the address labels and prepared them to go to the post office.

Ryan loved lunchtime so he said, "I'll get lunch after I go to the post office." You would never know he loved to eat by his slender physique, but lunch was the highlight of his day. Being health conscious, we shied away from greasy foods and stuck with deli sandwiches.

Couldn't Think Clearly That Evening

My brother Steve had a first birthday party for his fifth son, my godson, earlier in the evening. My wife was taking our son Britt to a hockey team party, so I tried to get Ryan to go with me to the party. I wanted to keep him from going out that night.

He struggled with this decision for quite a while. When it was time to leave, I started out the door, when I got into my van Ryan came out of the house and said he wanted to go with me.

He looked sharp in his black leather jacket, well-groomed hair, and great-smelling cologne. I backed down the driveway and pulled out of the cul-de-sac onto the street. When I got to the corner he said, "Stop, I cannot go.

Let me out." "What's wrong?" I said. "Who's going to be there?" He said, "Uncle Steve and his family, maybe Uncle Marty and Uncle Don's family." I told him I was not really sure who would be there. With that Ryan said he would go.

When I came to the strip mall behind our house, he said again, "I can't go." I said, "Come on, Ryan, cut this out. We are already running late." "Take me home," he said. So I turned into the strip mall and drove back to our house. When we got there he grabbed the door handle, but did not open it. "Maybe I'll go," He said. "Alright", I replied. "Let's go."

I drove out of our subdivision another way. When we came to the first stop sign he said, "I've got to get out". He opened the door got out and began walking home. I watched him in my rearview mirror with a pain in my heart.

I was not sure if he was forcing himself to come, afraid I would try to take him to the psyche ward with a surprise attack, or if he truly desired to go. It was probably a little bit of both. He was so confused and paranoid he couldn't make up his mind.

He was acting a bit psychotic. Dr. Herbert Wagemaker, quoted earlier, says, "For patients in an acute psychotic state, the world can be a terrifying place where they can trust no one and a place where everything is beyond their control or understanding." (1)

Serious Indecisiveness

As I drove to my brother's house, I felt sad and upset about Ryan. I did not feel comfortable at the party, so after a few hours I headed for home.

I arrived home around 9:30 p.m. and Ryan was very

upset. He had rented two DVD's and could not get them open. Seeing a yellow tab on each of them, I called Blockbuster to ask why we could not open them. They said they must have forgotten to remove the locks on the cases. If my son would bring them back, they would open them and give us credit on a new rental. Ryan gladly returned them.

I hoped that he would come back home and watch the movies, but when he got a call about a party at a friend's apartment, he said he was going to go.

"It is 10:00 p.m.," I said, "why go out now? I am going to bed." "Dad," he said, "it is a Friday night. Why are you going to bed so early?" "Friday, Saturday, Monday," I said. "When you are my age, every night's the same." My rationale was to downplay his need to go out on a weekend night.

Something Was Brewing

From various conversations I had with Ryan, he believed a number of his friends thought he was "crazy." Obviously, that really bothered him. For years he prided himself on being extremely intelligent with great grades, highly athletic and the life of the party. He always had a lot of friends.

A few days earlier Britt, Ryan's younger brother and I were watching Monday Night Football. Ryan came running in and said, "Why are you two talking about me?" "We weren't talking about you," we said. "Yes you were! What did you say?" He replied. "Nothing," we said with a sigh.

Suddenly he said, "Who's outside? Did you hear that?" "Hear what?" I said. He then ran out of the front door barefoot and started talking, but no one was there.

This was a new phase and looking back, I think Ryan may have started to exhibit some psychotic behavior, "hearing voices." Perhaps the abrupt withdrawal from his medication, lithium, may have induced it. I could only guess.

Another Late Night Out

At 11:00 p.m., his cell phone rang, to signal his ride was out in front of the house. Ryan left and came right back in. He came up to our bedroom and hollered, "Mom," and I told him to be quiet because his mom was sleeping. "Mom has my ATM card in her purse," he said. She woke up and got her purse.

As Ryan started leaving again, I said to him, "Ryan be good tonight. Do not spend too much money and do not stay out too long. I love you." He turned, walked away, and left the house.

Screaming Those Dreaded Words

My wife and I then went to bed. It was 11:30 p.m. Very early in the morning, around 4:45 a.m. I felt her get out of bed to check on Ryan and make sure he was alright. Suddenly, I heard her screaming, *"Ryan hung himself! Ryan hung himself!"* Being disabled I was unable to get out of bed and run downstairs to help. I felt my heart pounding so fast I could hardly breathe.

I grabbed the cell phone that I kept next to my bed and dialed 911. I told them to send an ambulance because my son had hung himself in the basement. The operator told me to stay on the line, but I told her I couldn't. I hung up and called my son Andy, but he did not answer.

In desperation I called my neighbor and told him what happened. I asked him to come over and help me get dressed, out of bed, and into my wheelchair scooter.

I prayed the paramedics would get there in time to revive my son.

Hysteria, Panic, and Numbness

After I called my neighbor I heard Joni from the basement: "Should I cut him down?" She was screaming. "Yes." I said. She looked for a kitchen knife. "Is he still alive?" I yelled down. She said nothing. I wondered, "Would mouth to mouth or CPR bring him back?" I waited anxiously to hear any word that there was a sign of life. It was too late.

Later Joni told me she was frantically trying to figure out what to do. It is a most surreal and horrific time anyone can experience, discovering the dead body of a loved one, especially a suicide victim.

When my neighbor arrived, I could hardly wait to get to the main floor and see Ryan. I quickly got dressed and into my scooter. I sped down my ramp into the kitchen feeling helpless. I saw the paramedics run downstairs and I called down there, "Is he alive?" No one said a word. What a helpless feeling being unable to see your own son, now dead. I yelled downstairs, "Can you bring up his body now?" They said, "No, we have to wait for the investigators and coroner."

Never Thought This Day Would Happen

Everything seemed like it was in a slow motion dream. I

kept thinking I would wake up and all this would be over. Never did I imagine my dear Ryan could end his life. His mother and I worked so hard, so long, lovingly taking him to doctors, counselors and rehabs. We made sure his medications were current, always reminding him to take them. I felt like God gave me Ryan as a mission to protect him, to keep him alive. I felt like a field commander who failed his mission by loosing a brother in battle. I kept thinking and saying "No Ryan, No! I can't believe you are gone."

He was alive one moment and gone the next. Grief plunged us into a myriad of emotions, from deep sadness and regret to guilt and hopelessness.

I thought, "How could this have happened on my watch? Did I do a terrible job as a parent? Why couldn't I have done more to help him? What will people think of him and us now?"

We heard nothing in his voice that he was contemplating suicide that day and suspected nothing. Time and again, for four years, he had gone to the edge and stopped before falling off the cliff.

Confronting His Friends

The next day we tried to piece together Ryan's last hours on earth through talking with his friends. We discovered he had gone to a party where there were many of his friends and Ryan confronted them about the rumor that he was "crazy." His friends told us they kept telling him they didn't say he was crazy.

Apparently that upset Ryan and he became very annoyed with them. One of Ryan's friends drove him home around 2:40 a.m. He told us Ryan sat in the car not wanting to get out. He asked his friend to stay out longer, but he told him he had to get home.

I wonder if Ryan thought, "If my friends are not saying I am crazy, maybe I really am going crazy!" I know he could never accept that way of thinking. He would rather die than believe he might be going crazy. He was very proud of his intelligence, wit and reasoning abilities. "How painful it must be to think you are loosing the respect of your peers?" He lived for his friends and valued their relationships.

An Act of Desperation

A million thoughts and feelings raced through my mind. I felt numb and half dead. At first glance Ryan left no note; he had said nothing about suicide to any of the friends he saw that night. How could this have happened?

In a book titled, "Out of the Nightmare", author David L. Conry, Ph.D., says, "Suicide is not chosen; it happens when pain exceeds resources for coping with pain. As in other forms of death, the victim of suicide dies if enough trauma is suffered or if life support systems are withdrawn or give out. An analogy to suicide is to imagine weights being piled onto a person's shoulders. Regardless of physical, emotional or moral qualities, the person will eventually collapse." (2)

Ryan had suffered tremendous amounts of emotional pain and trauma, which caused him to self-destruct.

Driven To Be Free

Ryan wanted to be free of these horrendous burdens and saw no other way out. I'm sure he hoped God would welcome him into heaven. I believe the Lord did understand what he was going through and was with him all the way.

I do not know what thoughts raced through my son's mind that night, I can only speculate. Sometimes I try to think about what he might have been thinking. What would make him decide to leave his loving dad, mom, and brothers? Did he comprehend fully that if he hung himself he would be gone from us on this earth forever?

Couldn't he have turned back and changed his mind? Couldn't he have waited until he had a nice long sleep and see if he felt better in the morning? Why didn't he run up to my room and scream, "Dad, I'm going to kill myself! What should I do? Can you help me?" All these questions and so many more, were gnawing at me. Why? Why? Why?

Irreversible Action

The results of a suicide cannot be reversed. There is no medicine, machine or miracle that can bring a troubled soul back to life. He was gone into eternity. He was so young, helpless, loving, caring and yet so hurting, confused, so filled with pain and desperation. I wish I could have said that one last goodbye and told him how much I loved him. I yearned to have been able to give him one last hug, one last kiss. To say one last time, "I love you." But I did not know the last time I saw him would be my last time I'd ever see him alive on this earth. This was no fairy-tale ending.

The suicide of a young adult is an unbearable pain for a parent. It is unnatural and flies in the face of what parenting is all about. Loving parents exist to help their offspring to be happy, fulfilled and to find their place in life. That existence is shaken to its core with the suicide of a child.

Irrational Thinking

When a person with a mental disorder commits the final act of suicide, it is not he or she who takes his or her own life rationally and in a premeditated fashion. The disorder takes over and completes the act.

For those suffering with bipolar, suicide can appear to be a solution especially if attempted as an act of anger or frustration. Most may not even be able to comprehend if the suicidal attempt succeeds there's no coming back. In golf terminology, "there is no mulligan with suicide." That is why it is so essential to take bipolar seriously. It is not something that will go away with time. Medication and therapy is not a guarantee that an individual with this disorder is ever "out of the woods." In fact my gut feeling and experience is the medical community is not prepared or able to effectively deal with these chronic, life-long mood illnesses.

They say, "How long can we hospitalize someone with a mental illness?" Many of the permanent or long-term mental health facilities are a thing of the past. So those who suffer are often on their own or family and friends must help them, if fortunate.

All Too Often Story Repeated

I was told about a middle-aged man, who was very active in his church and held a good job, who became seriously depressed. Two of his best childhood friends attend the church I pastor. They told me their friend took 10-12 sleeping pills and went out on a drive hoping he'd be killed in an accident. He fell asleep behind the wheel, became injured and was hospitalized. After interviewing and accessing him, they realized he was suicidal and committed him to the psyche ward. They kept him a week or so and then felt he was well enough to go home and released him. The next day, in the privacy of his home, he swallowed the 4 bottles of pills they gave him and died. How often does this scenario repeat itself? Sadly I believe the answer is, many times.

No Suicide Note

We looked all over to see if Ryan left us a note. We found none. Statistics have shown few with bipolar leave suicide notes. Most people like our son do not take their life because of an immediate problem, disappointment, or tragedy. Those with certain stages of bipolar can approach the brink of a place where suicide becomes the only way of stopping their pain.

In the book, "Night Falls Fast," written by Dr. Kay Redfield Jamison, she states, "Suicide is a particularly awful way to die; the mental suffering leading up to it is usually prolonged and intense. There is no morphine equivalent to ease the acute pain, and death not uncommonly is violent and grisly. The suffering of the suicide is private and inexpressible, leaving family members, friends, and colleagues to deal with an almost unfathomable kind of loss, as well as guilt. Suicide carries in its aftermath a level of confusion and devastation that is, for the most part, beyond description." (3)

The Pain of Unceasing Thoughts

Everyday people who lose a loved one to suicide experience a flood of thoughts about why it happened. They keep thinking, "Why did they do such a thing?" It seems virtually impossible to come to any closure. To put the suicide of your child or spouse behind you is virtually impossible.

It is something you must learn to cope with the rest of your life. It is more a matter of surviving each day. One day at a time, sometimes even one minute or even one second at a time. They say that, "time heals all wounds." It may be true that the passing of time helps assuage the grief. Maybe it does get a little easier to bear but every day the thoughts of your lost loved one pop up inadvertently, both good thoughts and painful ones.

Out of nowhere you find your eyes filling up with tears. Yet day by day, year by year, with the help of family, friends and faith, you hope the pain will start to diminish. If you are fortunate, you find yourself going on with your life.

It is painful to keep going through the "If only I..." syndrome. "If only I did or didn't do this or that."

I keep thinking, "Why did my son have to take his own life?" I was with him the entire day before. We worked together, accomplished things, shared a nice lunch, and talked about normal things.

I wonder if I should have looked for more signs that he was contemplating taking his own life that night. I wonder if he had been thinking about ending his life earlier that day. Maybe it was a spur-of- the-moment twisted thought. It could have been an overwhelming sense of paranoia or a manifestation of a psychotic or schizophrenic burst in the brain from a chemical imbalance.

If only we would have heard him when he came home and awakened. Why didn't we hear him come in that night, as we usually did, for all of our sons?

I try to imagine what my son was thinking about in the hours prior to his death. It did not appear he had thought this all out. He did not go out and buy a rope. He used one that had been in our basement for years, part of a weight-lifting apparatus.

The beam he threw the rope over was barely high enough for him to dangle without his feet touching the floor. He had to bend his knees to choke off the air to his brain. Why didn't he panic and stop? He could have pushed himself up on his toes, loosened the rope, and screamed for help. Why was he so determined to leave this life? He knew we loved him. He knew we would be devastated. Or did he? Or was he too determined to end his pain, that nothing else entered his mind?

When a loved one dies from a disease, accident, or random act of violence, it is painful and traumatic for the survivors. To seek closure is imperative for recovery and healing. But it appears to me that suicide brings a different grief process. Survivors do their best to cope, with the Lord's grace and strength, but I don't believe there is ever closure to a suicide.

People have advised me to let go of my son, to leave his death in the past, to realize God has everything under control, that somehow God's purposes will still be accomplished. My son is in heaven and we will see him again. I understand all this in my head, but my heart is still questioning if only I…...

After all is said and done, this appears to be our cross to bear. It is a burden no one volunteers to carry. It is an ongoing grief that confronts me every day. I hear a song that reminds me of my loved one, or a place we visited once before, a food he liked or a fragrant smell brings him back to my mind. I see a person who looks like Ryan, or someone says something, maybe just one word that triggers past memories. Each second, each minute, each day is a journey that I travel as I learn to survive the nightmare that claimed my son.

Suicide: A Serious Health Problem

Thirty thousand people take their lives by suicide every year in our country. That does not include the thousands of people who attempt, unsuccessfully, to take their own lives. How do we find a remedy for this? New medications and treatments are needed to slow down this alarming epidemic that is destroying many lives and families. I pray fervently that doctors, psychiatrists, pharmacists, and scientists will continue to discover successful treatments to deal with mood disorders and prevent suicide

Kenneth Dignan

Chapter Six

A Funeral Message from Dad

The day after Ryan's death, December 15, 2002, I got up early to get ready for church, as I did every Sunday, but this day was different. Instead of church, we had to go to the funeral home and cemetery to make arrangements for our son's burial. I awoke watching Pastor Charles Stanley, a national television preacher who was reading a scripture verse out of Hebrews 4:15-16, "For we do not have a high priest who is unable to sympathize with out weaknesses, but we have one who has been tempted in every way, just as we are-yet without sin. Let us then approach the throne of grace with confidence, so that we may receive mercy and find grace to help us in our time of need." (1)

As I reflected on that verse, I sensed a special presence of the Lord, as if God were speaking to my heart. Vivid thoughts rolled over in my head. I could not wait to get downstairs and put them down on paper.

I knew the Lord wanted me to share these thoughts at my son's memorial service, but I did not know if I could do that. My grief and my pain were so deep that it hurt just to breathe. The Lord assured me He would give me the strength and grace to preach this message.

Since the church I pastor does not own a church facility yet and we rent a school for Sunday morning services, I asked a pastor friend from a neighboring community if we could hold the service at his church. In case I had second thoughts about being too emotional to handle the message he said he would share the message, if I felt unable to deliver it.

On Tuesday, December 17, 2002, we got to the church at 9:00 a.m. for the family visitation prior to the public wake scheduled for 9:30 a.m.

Family members went up to the casket and viewed our son's body. Many tears and hugs were shared by all. I saw many of Ryan's aunts, uncles and young cousins sobbing. It all still felt like a terrible dream. I parked my motorized wheelchair at the head of the casket and often stroked my dear son's hair.

We were amazed at the steady flow of concerned individuals who came to pay their respects to Ryan and to his family. A constant line of people extended out of the church and into the parking lot until around 11:30 a.m. The two-hour receiving line totaled close to one thousand people.

The service began with an opening prayer by one of the elders from Eagle Rock Community Church, where I am pastor. Our music director led us in some inspirational choruses that lifted our hearts in worship. The three songs I chose were "The Power of Your Love," "The Heart of Worship," and "Draw Me Close."

Following the singing, a few other ministers shared prayer and scripture verses. Finally, the time came for the message I felt the Lord inspired me to write.

While I shared this message, I noticed almost one hundred young adults, all friends of Ryan's, seated to my left. They listened closely to every word.

The following thoughts are from my message:

The Lord felt my Son's Pain

The Lord was with Ryan every step of his journey. He knew my son would get bipolar, and He knew my son would suffer great emotional and mental pain. He knew this world was not a perfect place and that bad things happen to His children. He reminded me to look toward heaven.

A Bible verse in Revelation 21:4 says, "He will wipe away every tear from their eyes. There will be no more death, or mourning, or crying or pain; for the old order of things has passed away."

Jesus sympathized and identified with Ryan's pain. On the cross the Father laid on Jesus all of our sins and illnesses. Isaiah 53:6 says, "All we like sheep and gone astray and the Lord has laid on Him the Iniquity of us all." Isaiah 53:4-5 says, "He has borne our grief and carried our sorrows. He was wounded for our transgressions, bruised for our iniquities, the chastisement that will make us whole was on him and we are healed with his pain."

Hebrews 4:15 says, "We do not have a high priest who cannot sympathize with our weaknesses." The Lord Jesus Christ lived on this earth and He experienced pain. He knows everything about the human condition.

My son, Ryan loved the Lord. He had a tender heart for the things of God. Even in his illness he kept reaching out to the Lord. Just a week before he died he was in church and told me, "Dad that was a good sermon." I remember watching him bow his head as I prayed at the conclusion of my sermon.

I would often get him to tune into the Christian radio stations and we would talk about some of the new contemporary songs. He began to become more familiar with them.

The Lord Knew Ryan's Depression
Ryan had many times of doubt and confusion. He would often wonder why God allowed him to have bipolar. In Kings 19:1 Jezebel said, "Tell Elijah I will destroy him as he destroyed my prophets of Baal." Elijah showed great fear and ran for his life. He ran a day's journey into the wilderness and then sat down under a broom tree and asked God that he might die. He said, "Enough now, O Lord, take away my life." 2 Kings 2:11 says, "A chariot of fire and horses took Elijah up." Elijah experienced depression.

Matthew 11:2-3 says, "When John heard in prison about the works of Christ, he sent his disciples and said to Him, Are you the coming one or do we look for another?" Here we see when God delays answering a prayer, it can lead to doubt. John the Baptist was in prison, wondering why he had been left there. What was Jesus doing?

Mental illness is a cruel diagnosis. Its sufferers are often labeled crazy, lazy, or weak. Society says, "Snap out of it," "mind over matter," "if you believe, you will receive." Yet the mind can get sick just like the body. A physical illness can be seen through x-rays or blood tests, but mental illness is distinguishable only through abnormal actions or reactions, moods, inability to function or cope normally, etc.

When the disciples saw a blind man, they judged that he was blind because he or someone in his family sinned. Many feel that sicknesses or tragedies are a sign from God that you have done wrong, but Jesus dispelled that belief. John 9:2 says, "They saw a blind man, who sinned this man or his parents? Jesus said neither this man nor his parents sinned, but that the glory of God should be revealed in him."

A number of things shout at me from this passage:

1. This world can be a painful place. Sin and evil can bring havoc to the world. We wrestle not against flesh and blood but principalities of darkness. (Eph. 6:10-17)

2. This world is not what God wants. Sin and evil fill it. Jesus fought this painful world and experienced great sadness and pain. At Lazarus's death "Jesus wept bitterly." He was rejected, misunderstood, mocked, and crucified. (John 11:33-37)

3. This world is not fair but God will intervene in the end. Romans 8:22-23 says, "For we know that the whole creation groans and labors with birth pangs together until now. And not only they, but we also groan within ourselves, eagerly waiting for the adoption, the redemption of the body." Sin causes this world to decay and experience pain and suffering. It is a reminder of what happened when mankind disobeyed God's plan.

4. This world is temporary. 2 Corinthians 4:16-18, 5:1-4 says, "We do not lose heart. Though our outer nature is wasting away, our inner nature is

being renewed. We should not look at the things that are seen, but to the things that are unseen, for the things that are seen are temporary, but the things that are unseen are eternal. We know if our earthly body breaks down we have a new body from God. For we groan. We sign with anxiety longing to get out of these mortal lives to receive the immortal life." All humanity is wasting away. Our outer, earthly nature is temporary, frail, and dying. But each person has a spiritual nature that is dormant until God touches it and makes it alive eternally through faith in Jesus Christ.

The Lord Loved Ryan Unconditionally
God loves us. He showed His love by sending His only begotten Son, Jesus Christ, to die on the cross to purchase our salvation. He came to die for people who hated, blasphemed, and rejected His name.

Romans 5:8 says, "God demonstrated His own love toward us, in that while we were still sinners, Christ died for us."

John 3:16 says, "For God so loved the world that He gave His only Son that whoever would believe in Him would not perish but have everlasting life."

I sensed the Lord whispering to my heart and impressing these thoughts on my mind: "As much as you and your wife loved your son Ryan, I loved him even more. Ryan is my child. He knew me as His Savior and Lord. His mind chemistry was out of balance, and he did not know what to think or how to think. His mind was tortured and he felt he had to come home to heaven. He released himself to me and I took him home."

I fully realize life is a precious gift. It's dangerous to decide to end a life in a moment of despair. If you find yourself feeling these things talk to your parents, friends, teachers, and counselors immediately. The Lord can help you.

More than once Ryan asked me, "If I killed myself would I go to hell?" I would always say, "God gave you a precious life and He does not want you to give up."

God would not let anything separate my son from his love. Not evil powers or "anything else in all creation." (Romans 8:38-39)

Romans 8:28 states, "God causes all things to work together for the good of those who love Him those called according to His purpose."

In God's permissive will, He can allow a terrible thing to happen, even if He does not cause it, for a deeper purpose than may be revealed in this life.

This can even be true with an untimely death of a loved one. I believe God knew Ryan was going to commit suicide.

God allowed a terrible tragedy to be inflicted on all of Job's sons and daughters. In this terrible attack Job prayed, "The Lord gives and the Lord takes away. Blessed be the name of the Lord." (Job 1:21) It is hard to believe a loving God could allow a storm to kill all the children of a man of God. But it happened. Why? We do not really know other than to test Job. The Bible assures us that God works in strange and mysterious ways.

King David's son Absalom was killed when his neck

was broken after his hair got tangled in a tree limb while riding a horse. Samson's strength returned long enough for him to pull down the pillars that killed him. Judas was overwhelmingly depressed after he betrayed Jesus, so he hung himself.

When Jesus was on the cross He prayed for the ones who were crucifying Him. "Father, forgive them for they do not know what they are doing (Luke 24:34). The Lord said to my heart, "In Ryan's despair, I forgave him, for due to his illness, he did not know what he was doing."

What the enemy of our souls meant for evil, the Lord turned out for good by taking my son home to heaven where he would be free of his torment and pain. He was ushered right into the presence of the Lord Jesus Christ in Heaven.

In July of 2002, at the New Life Clinic, Ryan composed a poem during his twenty-eight days there at the rehab center. It is almost prophetic:

28 DAYS AHEAD
By Ryan Lee Dignan
My actions brought me to this time
Where punishment fits the crime.
My addictions don't matter anymore
'Cause death's come knockin' at my door.
What lies in these days ahead I do not know?
But if not changed, life will deal that fatal blow.
Take this journey day by day.
If it directs light, then that's the way.
God is the path I need to take.
What if in the end I fall and break?

Will You pick me up and help me walk again?
I know You will ----- you're my best friend.
28 days to change my ways.
28 days to escape this maze.
28 days to find my soul.
28 days to reach that goal.
I can see it now, the good life's here.
I live my hours with no fear.
Temptations don't faze me anymore.
'Cause when Satan came a-knockin' at my door.
I turned my cheek and felt for him no more.
Thank You God, You are the One
Who broke my sin; now life's just begun.
28 days saved my life.
28 days of pain and strife.
28 days, here I am.
28 days God's in command.

This poem was read at the funeral. It had a powerful impact on all who heard it.

After the poem was read, the music director of our church, sang a song that Ryan and I loved to listen to together by Mark Schultz. Here are the words:

HE'S MY SON

I'm down on my knees again tonight.
I'm hoping this prayer will turn out right.
See, there is a boy that needs your help.
I've done all that I can do myself.
His mother is tired.
I'm sure you can understand.

Each night as he sleeps
She goes in to hold his hand
And she tries not to cry
As the tears fill her eyes.
Can you hear me?
Am I getting through tonight?
Can you see him?
Can you make him feel all right?
If you can hear me
Let me take his place somehow.
See, he's not just anyone,
He's my son.
Sometimes late at night I watch him sleep.
I dream of the boy he'd like to be.
I try to be strong and see him through.
But God, who he needs right now is You.
Let him grow old,
Live life without fear.
What would I be
Living without him here?
He's so tired and he's scared.
Let him know that You're there.
Can you hear me?
Can you see him?
Please don't leave him.
He's my son.

Mark Schultz Music/BMI (2)

Questions Unanswered on Earth

We ask, "How could God let something as bad as this happen? Why didn't He stop Ryan?" But we do not know what is going on behind the scenes in the spiritual realm.

In the Bible, Job had no clue as to why all of his sons and daughters were killed. He did not know there was a war in heaven between God and Lucifer. Would Job still trust the Lord if tragedy struck his family? Satan said no. God said he would. We know the rest of the story.

Job was in grief and pain. Yet he did not lose his faith or trust in God. Tragedy can make God seem uncaring and distant. But in the midst of suffering and death, God can break through and show us what really matters.

I would love to have Ryan back, but deep down in my heart I have a peace that Ryan is with Jesus, and He will use this pain I have to bring glory to His broader plan.

Upon sharing this message, I led in a prayer for everyone at the memorial ceremony to be open to receiving God's comfort, peace and strength. I prayed for each person to ask Christ into their hearts and receive eternal life and forgiveness for their sins. I mentioned I did not believe Ryan's death would be in vain but that many would be inspired to become stronger in their relationship with God in honor of him.

Kenneth Dignan

Chapter Seven

Reflecting on My Life Experiences

Ryan remarked to me many times how bad he felt that I had a disability from polio. He often told me how much he respected me for doing so much with my limited mobility and physical challenges.

He knew I had fought many physical, spiritual, and emotional battles in my life. I learned early in life that adversity is no respecter of persons. Life is not fair; some go through frequent difficulties while others enjoy a smooth life.

Suffering: A Way of Life

For as long as I can remember, pain, suffering, and discomfort have been a part of my life. It was not easy growing up with physical weaknesses and a disability. I suffered through many surgeries, therapy sessions and pain throughout my childhood. I could have become paralyzed, unable to stand or walk at all. I could have even died an early death, yet God kept me around.

I had to wear braces on my legs. I used springs on my highchair to move my arms up and down. I have never been able to dress myself. Someone has always had to assist me with my toiletries.

I needed four major reconstructive surgeries on my shoulders and left leg before I was ten years old. I could not walk long distances. I needed help getting out of a chair, climbing stairs and if I fell to the ground, I could not get up on my own.

Going through the teen years was even more difficult trying to feel accepted in spite of my deformed right arm and hunchback. I walked with a limp and my friends had to push me around in a little red wagon as a child and wheelchair as a teenager, because I could not wheel myself.

Relied on Past Experiences

I had a loving family who were very supportive, but their love and support did not take away my longing to be normal. I tried to play neighborhood sports by sitting on a chair and hitting baseballs, or sitting on a stool parked in front of a hockey net as a goalie. My father took me to high school football games, as he was a volunteer assistant coach for a childhood friend, who was the head coach at a Catholic high school in the Chicago area. I would often cry as I sat in the stands because I longed to be able to play football.

That is why I so enjoyed seeing Ryan love and play high school football. It thrilled me to see him enjoy athletics. I was very proud of him as he worked tirelessly in Pop Warner football and then play both offense and defense, in high school, as a freshman and sophomore.

Along with sports, I developed a deep love and talent for music and convinced my dad to buy me a set of drums.

I sat behind them and learned to play. That led me into numerous rock bands in the sixties when rock music was evolving. Ryan picked up my love for music.

Since Ryan's suicide, I have had to rely heavily on all I've learned from my experiences to help me make it through each day, one step at a time.

Occasionally little things about Ryan remind me of many wonderful memories about him. Though towards the end of his life there were more tough times than good, the good memories about Ryan's life far outweigh the painful ones.

Ryan Impacted Lives

At the funeral, one young man told me my son had, "helped him more than anyone else in his life." He said, "Ryan always knew how to cheer me up."

Another friend of Ryan's, who knew him at college, wrote this:

> *Dear Dignan Family,*
> *My deepest sympathy goes out to all of you. I can't imagine your world without Ryan. He was always a good friend to me at Western Illinois University. He had a special gift of making people laugh and be happy when they were down, and for that, he will always be remembered. May God be with you all at this time of mourning.*
> *Sincerely, Dan (from Palatine, Illinois)*

Not More Than You Can Bear?

I have often asked God not to give me more than I could

bear. Sometimes I would bargain with the Lord and say, "You allowed me to get polio and become disabled. Please let that be my heaviest cross to bear." But there are many mysteries with the way God works. Even though a verse in the Bible says, "God works all things together for our good." (1) I have been puzzled often about how this can happen. But deep down I know God has our life in His hands.

Trying to Understand Prayer

I remember praying a sincere, tearful prayer a few days before his death, for God to touch my son and heal him. I know that answers to prayer are far more complicated than having God grant me my wish like a genie in a bottle. But my wife and I were exhausted with fighting the battle to save our son's life.

Almost immediately, after I prayed, I heard my son talking to his mother. He got upset and threw a drink coaster at the wall in the living room. Then I was jolted by a loud smash down the hall. Ryan had punched his fist through a hollow door. He was truly on edge the last week of his life.

To make sense of all this I had to conclude that sometimes God delays in answering our prayers the way we want Him too. This is a painful lesson to understand because either He sees a bigger picture or there are mysteries in His will we cannot understand in this life. During those times I am tempted to think, "Why pray? I prayed for Ryan and God did not answer. Ryan died."

We may also feel God answers the prayers of others and not ours. We must be doing something wrong. I've had to come to the conclusion that the Bible teaches us prayer is more than asking God for favors. Prayer is a word which describes the act of communicating with the Lord whether through meditating on scriptures, talking to Him about your life and concerns, or even just sitting in silence in His presence.

God calls us to pray and ask for things. As we see in Luke 11:9 which states, "Ask and it will be given to you." Yet every prayer should echo the words Jesus prayed in the garden of Gethsemane in Matthew 26:39 when He said, "My Father, if it is possible, may this cup be taken from me. Yet not as I will, but as you will." Similar to the Lord's Prayer, "Thy kingdom come, Thy will be done."

Handling Self Doubt and Inadequacies

Another area I had to deal with while Ryan was going through all this was personally staying strong while dealing with doubt and guilt. I struggled with the scripture that speaks about the qualifications of a minister in 1Timothy 3:4-5. "He must be one who manages his own household well, keeping his children under control with all dignity." (If a man does not know how to manage his own household, how will he take care of the church of God?)

This passage of scripture caused me to do a lot of soul searching to see if I was still qualified to serve as a minister. Having four active, strong-willed sons created many times of stress. I felt my wife and I did everything we could to prepare our children to grow into mature, caring, Christian young men. Yet there were very challenging times that took a lot of prayer, discipline and persistence.

I wondered what people in the church would think of

me. Would they say, "How can he teach what God wants me to do when he could not even help his own son deal successfully with bipolar? How can a good minister have a son who would end his life by suicide?

I felt like running away to Florida where no one knew me. When Ryan died my grief was beyond what I could bear. I wondered if I could face people with all the pain I felt inside. The same grace from God that helped me love and deal with Ryan while he went through his disorder became the same grace that helped me continue ministering as a pastor after my son died.

Ministers have to set a good and moral example. They need to exhibit love, compassion, and forgiveness. Fortunately, they do not have to be perfect. There are numerous illustrations in the Bible of saints God used who were far from perfect. Abraham fathered Ishmael with Hagar, who was not his wife. Jacob stole Esau's birthright. King David committed adultery with Bathsheba and conspired to have her husband killed. (Genesis 16, 27; 2 Samuel 11-12)

I am not trying to minimize what sin can do. Many sad and destructive experiences can result from sin. That is where God's grace, compassion, and forgiveness come in. Jesus said, "He who is without sin throw the first stone." (John 8:7)

I came to the conclusion that being able to lead and guide a child between the ages of two and sixteen is a lot different than trying to force a child age sixteen or older to participate in spiritual things against their will. The passage in 1 Timothy 3 had to be referring to managing your children while they are truly children. Not older teens or adults.

How Could He Leave Us?

It is unbelievable trying to deal with the death of a loved one from suicide. It seems like you go over and over many instances where you think what else could I have done to prevent this? Days prior to his death I definitely noticed Ryan had become more agitated and frustrated. I thought, "Here we go again." Had I known that he would commit suicide a few days later, I would have called the authorities and had him put in a mental health center. He would have hated me for a while, but seeing my son in a psychiatric ward for however long, would have been better than seeing him take his own life.

Grief and Trauma

An author named Albert Y. Hsu, who lost his father to suicide, wrote a book titled, "Grieving a Suicide." In it he says, "Suicide heightens the agony of loss. Different kinds of loss are grieved differently. The loss of a child, for instance, brings a different sort of grief than the loss of a spouse or an elderly parent. Each kind of death raises its own issues. A teen's death brings feelings of regret that a life of budding potential was cut short; the death of a wife or husband may leave the surviving spouse struggling with the challenges of widowhood and single parenting. Each of these losses is difficult even in the most 'normal of circumstances;' suicide complicates and intensifies each grief. What would already be a heartbreaking teen death becomes even more tragic as a teen suicide. How a family grieves for a teen's suicide may look very different from grief over a grandfather's suicide." (2)

He goes on to say that traumatic grief is not a linear process mapped out from one starting point to a final destination. Rather, it is a journey filled with twists and turns, unexpected detours and dead ends that force us back over ground we thought we had already covered. Often several different, overlapping emotions may assault us at once and we find ourselves caught in cycles of good days and bad.

No Hollywood Script

Everyone likes a movie or story with a happy ending where everyone lived "Happily ever after." Sadly, life for some can be so unbearable that the only way to find relief is suicide. Those of us without a chemical imbalance in our brain can hardly grasp that.

A few people have said, "Don't feel bad. Be happy Ryan is with Jesus" or "You can't keep thinking about him, it will only make things worse. Remember the good times with your son, and as time goes by, it will get easier."

Such statements seem so shallow. I miss my son greatly and I never want to get over him not being here with us. The death of a loved one is hard, but suicide has a unique pain all its own.

As if He Never Lived

Joni told me recently that since our son's death she had been feeling especially depressed about Ryan and struggled to complete even the simplest of tasks, housework, filing or gardening. Perhaps if Ryan died from natural causes people would talk more freely about him. She mentioned to someone at a party that she was down and the person looked at her without responding and then walked away, apparently uncomfortable about getting involved in a conversion regarding our son's suicide.

At the support group called LOSS (Loved Ones of Survivors of Suicide), we learned it was important to keep talking about your loved one. Celebrate their birthday, do something memorable on the day they died, honor them every Christmas, visit their grave often and appreciate who they were, a gift from God, if only for a brief time.

When you go through trials like these I can see you lean heavily on all the wisdom or insights you've gained from all your life experiences. In my case I feel like I've had as many challenging experiences as anyone can handle.

Chapter Eight

Lessons to Be Learned

Here are lessons and observations I have made that can help individuals who may be suicidal due to bipolar, along with guidance to their family and friends. Hopefully some of them can be beneficial to get them through their hurt and pain from mood disorders. These are steps to consider if you suspect bipolar or have already been diagnosed with it.

Act on Initial Signs

If you see a loved one swinging from one extreme mood to another, depression, fits of rage, extreme anxiety, etc. Depending on their age, either mention it to your doctor right away or encourage them to do it themselves.

Deal Immediately with Alcohol and Drug Use

If you find out your loved one is abusing drugs or alcohol, do not accept it just because "everybody" does it. Tell them about the dangers of substance abuse, and the brain damage that can occur from upsetting chemicals in the mind and body.

For a teenager, it can be hard to get through to your kids about this, but never give up keeping your eyes on your children. It is also difficult to get help for adults with this disorder.

If alcoholism, drug addiction, or mood disorders run in your family, do not cover it up and wish it away. Don't be afraid to seek the help of a mental health professional.

Let your loved one know there are good reasons to live soberly. How many smokers, drinkers, and drug users wish they had never started?

Follow Professional Advice

If you or a loved one is diagnosed with bipolar, find a trained, qualified and proven professional to assist you. Seek out a psychiatrist, psychologist, therapist and pharmacist you feel comfortable with and have received solid recommendations about their work. Make sure they are available, return phone calls promptly, spend adequate time talking to you about the disorder, medications and treatments, and are willing to try something else if things are not working or getting better. Stick with them and follow all their advice.

Take medications prescribed for you. There are many medications out there, so it takes time to discover the correct ones for your body and mind. Keep working with your doctors as they continue to adjust the medications.

Find a Good Support System

Find a support group, church group, youth group, or even just a few close friends you can share with and lean on for a listening ear and advice. You can search the Web, call hospitals, and ask psychiatrists and other professionals if they know of any support groups.

Our best support came from a small group at our church, ten to fifteen people who met monthly. Their prayers and listening ears sustained us during our own horrible struggle, weeks and months after Ryan's death. They still help to this day.

We tried to find our son a support group, but his stubbornness defeated him. We suggested a few young adult groups at churches though he never gave enough time to develop relationships. He rarely attended AA meetings but when he did he said he did not feel accepted. We could not find a group he ever felt comfortable with.

We kept telling our son if he would get one or two people who were going through what he was, that he could be honest with, it could reinforce him greatly, especially if these friends quit substances and found healthy activities to be involved in.

A number of my son's friends came up to me after he died and said, "We didn't know what bipolar was and how it affected Ryan. Now we want to learn more about how to help someone who has bipolar." I shared with them the best thing to do was avoid substance abuse. Alcohol abuse and using illegal drugs was the worst thing you can do whether you have bipolar or not.

Be Creative
Bipolar often causes problems being able to complete high school or college. Be creative in your efforts to find the best plans that will enable you to achieve whatever goals you have. Creative schooling such as home tutoring, online classes, work study, GED, or a technical school might work best for you. If you are having a difficult time adjusting to high school and desire to finish and attend college do whatever it takes.

You may have a hard time finding a job that gives you the flexibility you need to allow for various moods, interrupted sleep patterns, and tiredness. The right medications can help and many jobs have flexible hours. The important thing is not the size of your paycheck or a top executive job. You can still have a successful and fulfilling career as you find your niche in the world.

Take things one step at a time and do not get discouraged. It is not easy, but if you build a support group around you of family, friends, and professionals, you can make it.

Do Not Take Suicidal Thoughts Lightly

If you ever think about taking your life, get help. Suicide is not the way out. Beware of drugs and alcohol because they increase suicidal thoughts. You may feel you have tried everything, but don't give up. Take each hour, each day, and each minute at a time.

You are special and important. Your life matters. Many people would miss you and never be the same if you decide to end your life.

Join a Good Church

Find a church with caring people who will help you grow in your faith. Study the Bible and learn how to pray. Your life is precious to God. He has a plan and purpose for your life. Remember you are not an accident.

If you are the parent, spouse, relative, or friend of someone who has bipolar, watch for suicidal tendencies, prolonged agitation, anger, depression, or ceasing to take medications. If you see these signs, do whatever you can to get that person to a hospital or treatment center as soon as possible. Do not wait until the suffering individual wants to get help.

Confront Twisted Thinking

My son's bipolar led him to believe he needed alcohol and drugs to numb his pain. He could drink with his friends, but was embarrassed to admit he had to take medication.

The doctor who performed his autopsy called me six weeks after Ryan's death with the toxicology report. There were no illegal drugs found in his system, but his blood alcohol level was 0.10.

Did alcohol cause Ryan to commit suicide? I do not believe so but I'm sure it did not help. Many times before, he had been higher than that limit when the police or hospitals tested him.

Our son seemed to have a death wish due to his disorder. His mother and I loved him. We prayed for him all the time. He went to church his whole life. He would tell people he had "perfect parents." Manic-depression can devastate a beautiful life and fill it with pain and agony.

Beware of Second Guessing

I wish I could turn back the clock and forcefully commit my son back in the hospital, even against his will. We knew he was a danger to himself so we kept trying to figure out when to take drastic actions. Whether it was putting him in the hospital, sending him to rehab, or nagging him to take all his meds and to stay away from substances, we know we did our best to help him. Yet there's always that problem of second guessing.

Deal With Misconceptions

Some Christians believe a person who abuses alcohol or drugs cannot be in a right relationship with God. Some even say that an individual using illegal substance cannot go to heaven. This is a touchy subject. Yes God desires His children to live a godly and holy life. But some of His children can be mentally or physically ill causing them to fall short.

As a minister with a bipolar son, I have had to lay preconceived theological beliefs aside and look deeper for a biblical understanding. I have come to see that the Bible teaches "All have sinned and fallen short of the glory of God." (Romans 3:23). Every human being sins and does things wrong. Anyone who believes in Christ can find forgiveness every time they sin by asking His blood which He shed on the cross to cleanse them. (1 John 1:9)

Certain individuals have a genetic predisposition to a chemical imbalance in their brain that can lead to various psychological disorders and addictions. These individuals are driven by their racing thoughts and cravings for substance. They can have profound religious experiences and then sink into depths of depression and despair. Only the Lord Himself can truly understand what these people go through. God is the final judge of who goes to heaven by the grace of Christ.

Some Christians believe that no one who commits suicide goes to heaven. They say any person who takes his/her own life is breaking the commandment, "Thou shall not kill." However the sixth commandment, "Thou shall not kill," is more accurately translated, "Thou shall not murder." Therefore, to say suicide is in the category of breaking the sixth commandment is not true.

I believe it is wrong to rank suicide with murder, theft, adultery, bearing false witness and coveting one's neighbor's property, as the 10 Commandments deal with. All those have evil intent, whereas suicide is usually an act of personal desperation.

If a person is caught in attempted murder, burglary, adultery, or perjury, they could be prosecuted. The least they could be accused of is committing a sin, because evil intent was still evident, even if the crime itself was stopped in time. If a person is caught attempting suicide, most people would interpret it as a personal cry for help, and try to provide such help.

When it comes to suicide God understands the mind of a confused, hurting individual, especially one who has a chemical imbalance or serious psychological illness. Suicide is a horrific and drastic way to die and everything must be done to prevent it.

In Paul's letter to the Ephesians he said, "We are saved by grace through faith, it is a gift from God, not by works so no one can boast." (Eph 2:8-9). God's grace and love is able "to cover a multitude of sins." (1 Peter 4:8)

Keep His Memory Alive
A task that helps me keep Ryan's memory alive is looking at pictures, talking about him, and reflecting on him.

If a song, television program, movie or location triggers his memory, I embrace it. We also sponsor an annual Ryan Dignan Memorial Concert once a year with contemporary Christian artists, and of course I wrote this book to keep Ryan's Story and memory alive.

A Heartfelt Prayer

Let me share with you a prayer I prayed to the Lord after Ryan died. "My dear Lord, how I wish I could have been allowed to bear my son's pain. It hurts me deeply to know how much he hurt. May I do whatever I can to care about others so they can learn from his suffering and gain understanding, healing, tolerance, and compassion for all who struggle with mental disorders. I do not believe his life was in vain. May you allow his story to be shared with many and cause them to trust in you more fully and receive eternal life through Jesus Christ your Son."

Chapter Nine

Shocking Statistics
and
Clear Symptoms

I've searched the Internet and read many books which contain helpful information along with numerous statistics and symptoms about bipolar disorder, mental illness, substance abuse, and suicide. Here are some of my findings.

The National Center for Health Statistics Suicide
(All figures are for U.S. in 2000)
Deaths Annually: 29,350 – 30,000
Death Rate: 10.7 deaths per 100,000
Cause of Death Rank: 11th

The American Foundation for Suicide Prevention
Over 30,000 people in the United States kill themselves every year.

Accounting for 1.3% of all deaths, suicide is the eleventh leading cause of death in the United States.

A person dies by suicide about every eighteen minutes in the United States. An attempt is made an estimated once a minute.

There are more than four male suicides for every

female suicide. However, at least twice as many females as males attempt suicide.

Every day, approximately eighty-six Americans take their own lives, and fifteen hundred attempt it. There are an estimated eight to twenty-five suicides attempts to one completion. (1)

Among Youth

Risk factors for suicide among youth include suicidal thoughts, psychiatric disorders (such as depression, impulsive aggressive behavior, bipolar disorder, certain anxiety disorders), drug and/or alcohol abuse and previous suicide attempts, with the risk increased if there is also access to firearms and situational stress.

Youth and Suicide

Suicide is the second leading cause of death among college-age students. (Ages 18 – 24)

Suicide attempts pose the greatest life-threatening danger for college women.

The rate of suicide among young males has tripled since 1970.

There are almost 1,100 suicides projected to occur on campuses this year.

Among college students, 7.5 of every 100,000 take their own lives.

4 out of 5 young adults who attempt suicide have given clear warnings.

18-24 year-olds think about suicide more often than any other age group and one in twelve U.S. College students makes a suicide plan.

Suicide is the third-leading cause of death among youth overall (ages 15-24)

Every hour and forty-five minutes another young person commits suicide.

The National College Health Risk Behavior Study found that 11.4% of students seriously consider attempt suicide.

In a present poll, up to 60% of high school students reported thinking about suicide at least once in their lives.

In 1998, suicide killed more young adults than AIDS, cancer, heart disease, pneumonia, birth defects, stroke, influenza and chronic lung disease combined.

Risk Factors

Mental Illness: 90% of adolescent suicide victims have at least one diagnosable, active psychiatric illness at the time of death – most often depression, substance abuse, and conduct disorders. Only 15% of suicide victims were in treatment at the time of death.

Previous Attempts: 26-33% of adolescent suicide victims have made a previous suicide attempt

Stressors: Suicide in youth often occurs after the victim has gotten into some sort of trouble or has experienced a recent disappointment or rejection.

Firearms: Having a firearm in the home greatly increases the risk of youth suicide. (2)

The American Academy of Child and Adolescent Psychiatry

Suicides among young people nationwide have increased dramatically in recent years. Each year in the U.S., thousands of teenagers commit suicide.

Teenagers experience strong feelings of stress, confusion, self-doubt, pressure to succeed, financial uncertainty, and other fears while growing up.

For some teenagers, divorce, the formation of a new family with step-parents and step-siblings, morbidity moving to a new community can be very unsettling and may intensify self-doubts. In some cases, suicide appears to be a "solution."

Depression and suicidal feelings are treatable mental disorders. The child or adolescent needs to have his or her illness recognized and diagnosed, and appropriate treatment plans developed. When parents are in doubt whether their child has a serious problem, a psychiatric examination can be very helpful.

Many of the symptoms of suicidal feelings are similar to those of depression.

Parents should be aware of the following signs of adolescents who may try to kill themselves:

- Change in eating and sleeping habits
- Withdrawal from friends, family, and regular activities
- Violent actions, rebellious behavior, or running away
- Drug and alcohol use
- Unusual neglect of personal appearance

- Marked personality change
- Persistent boredom, difficulty concentrating, or a decline in the quality of schoolwork
- Frequent complaints about physical symptoms, often related to emotions, such as stomachaches, headaches, fatigue, etc.
- Loss of interest in pleasurable activities
- Not tolerating praise or rewards.

A teenager who is planning to commit suicide may also:

- Complain of being a bad person or feeling "rotten inside"
- Give verbal hints with statements such as: "I won't be a problem for you much longer," "Nothing matters,"
- "It's no use," and "I won't see you again."
- Put his or her affairs in order; for example, give away favorite possessions, clean his or her room, throw away important belongings, etc.
- Become suddenly cheerful after a period of depression have signs of psychosis (hallucinations or bizarre thoughts).

If a child or adolescent says, "I want to kill myself" or "I'm going to commit suicide," always take the statement seriously. Seek evaluation from a psychiatrist or physician. People often feel uncomfortable talking about death. However, asking the child or adolescent whether he or she is depressed or thinking about suicide can be helpful. Rather than "putting thoughts in the child's head," such a question will provide assurance that somebody cares and will give the young person the chance to talk about the problems.

If one or more of these signs occurs, parents need to talk to their child about their concerns and seek professional help when the concerns persist. With support from family and professional treatment, children and teenagers who are suicidal can heal and return to a healthier path of development. (3)

The National Institute of Mental Health Questions About Suicide

What should you do if someone tells you they are thinking about suicide?

If someone tells you they are thinking about suicide, you should take their distress seriously, listen non-judgmentally, and help them get to a professional for evaluation and treatment. People consider suicide when they are hopeless and unable to see alternative solutions to their problems. Suicidal behavior is most often related to a mental disorder (depression) or to alcohol or other substance abuse. Suicidal behavior is also more likely to occur when people experience stressful events (major losses, incarceration). If someone is in imminent danger of harming himself or herself, do not leave the person alone. You may need to take emergency steps to get help, such as calling 911. When someone is in a suicidal crisis, it is important to limit access to firearms or other lethal means of committing suicide such as ropes, belts, sharp knives, and prescription or non-prescription drugs.

What biological factors increase risk for suicide?

Researchers believe that both depression and suicidal behavior can be linked to decreased serotonin in the brain. Low levels of a serotonin metabolite, 5-HIAA, have been detected in cerebral spinal fluid in persons who have attempted suicide, as well as by postmortem studies examining certain brain regions of suicide victims. One of the goals of understanding the biology of suicidal behavior is to improve treatments. Scientists have learned that serotonin receptors in the brain increase their activity in persons with major depression and suicidality, which explains why medications that desensitize or down-regulate these receptors (such as the serotonin reuptake inhibitors, or SSRI's) have been found effective in treating depression. Currently, studies are underway to examine to what extent medications like SSRI's can reduce or trigger suicidal behavior.

Can the risk for suicide be inherited?

There is growing evidence that familial and genetic factors contribute to the risk for suicidal behavior. Major psychiatric illnesses, including bipolar disorder, major depression, schizophrenia, alcoholism and substance abuse, and certain personality disorders, which run in families, increase the risk for suicidal behavior. This does not mean that suicidal behavior is inevitable for individuals with this family history; it simply means that such persons may be more vulnerable and should take steps to reduce their risk, such as getting evaluation and treatment at the first sign of mental illness.

Does depression increase the risk for suicide?

Although the majority of people who have depression do not die by suicide, having major depression does increase suicide risk compared to people without depression. The risk of death by suicide may, in part, be related to the severity of the depression. New data on depression that has followed people over long periods of time suggests that about two percent of those people ever treated for depression in an outpatient setting will die by suicide. Among those ever treated for depression in an inpatient hospital setting, the rate of death by suicide is four percent which is twice as high. Those treated for depression as in-patients following suicide ideation or suicide attempts are six percent about three times as those who were only treated as outpatients. There are also dramatic gender differences in lifetime risk of suicide in depression. Whereas about seven percent of men with a lifetime history of depression will die by suicide, only one percent of women with a lifetime history of depression will die by suicide.

Another way about thinking of suicide risk and depression is to examine the lives of people who have died by suicide and see what proportion of them were depressed. From that perspective, it is estimated that about sixty percent of people who commit suicide have had a mood disorder (e.g., major depression, bipolar disorder). Younger persons who kill themselves often have a substance abuse disorder in addition to being depressed.

Do alcohol and other drug abuse increase the risk for suicide?

A number of recent national surveys have helped shed

light on the relationship between alcohol and other drug use with suicidal behavior. A review of minimum-age drinking laws and suicides among youths age eighteen to twenty has found that lower minimum-age drinking laws was associated with higher youth suicide rates. In a large study following adults who drink alcohol, suicidal ideation was reported among persons with depression. In another survey, persons who reported that they had made a suicide attempt during their lifetime were more likely to have had a depressive disorder, and many also had an alcohol and/or substance abuse disorder. In a study of all non-traffic injury deaths associated with alcohol intoxication, over twenty percent were suicides.

In studies that examine risk factors among people who have completed suicide, substance use and abuse occurs more frequently among youth and adults, compared to older persons. For particular groups at risk, such as American Indians and Alaskan Natives, depression and alcohol use and abuse are the most common risk factors for completed suicide. Alcohol and substance abuse problems contribute to suicide behavior in several ways. Persons who are dependent on substances often have a number of other risk factors for suicide. In addition to being depressed, they are also likely to have social and financial problems. Substance use and abuse can be common among persons prone to be impulsive, and among persons who engage in many types of high-risk behaviors that result in self-harm. Fortunately, there are a number of effective prevention efforts that reduce risk for substance abuse in youth, and there are effective treatments for alcohol and substance use problems. Researchers are currently testing treatments specifically for persons with substance abuse problems who are also suicidal, or have attempted suicide in the past.

Is it possible to predict suicide? At the current time, there is no definitive measure to predict suicide or suicidal behavior. Researchers have identified factors that place individuals at higher risk for suicide, but very few persons with these risk factors will actually commit suicide. Risk factors include mental illness, substance abuse, previous suicide attempts, family history of suicide, history of being sexually abused, and impulsive or aggressive tendencies. Suicide is a relatively rare event and it is, therefore, difficult to predict which persons with these risk factors will ultimately commit suicide. (4)

These materials have opened up many insights to me as I have written this book. I hope they will add to your understanding as you try to come to grips with tragedy and pain.

The following is taken from a brochure of the National Mental Health Association on the Signs and Symptoms of bipolar disorder:

Bipolar Disorder - Signs and Symptoms

What are the symptoms of bipolar disorder? Bipolar disorder is often difficult to recognize and diagnose. It causes a person to have a high level of energy, grandiose thoughts or ideas, and impulsive or reckless behavior. These symptoms may feel good to a person, which may lead to denial that there is a problem.

Another reason bipolar disorder is difficult to diagnose

is that its symptoms may appear to be part of another illness or attributed to other problems, such as substance abuse, poor school performance, or trouble in the workplace.

Symptoms of Mania

- Excessive energy, activity, restlessness, racing thoughts and rapid talking.

- Denial that anything is wrong.

- Extreme "high" or euphoric feelings — a person may feel "on top of the world" and nothing, including bad news or tragic events, can change this "happiness."

- Easily irritated or distracted.

- Decreased need for sleep – an individual may last for days with little or no sleep without feeling tired.

- Unrealistic beliefs in one's ability and powers — a person may experience feelings of exaggerated confidence or unwarranted optimism. This can lead to overly ambitious work plans and the belief that nothing can stop him or her from accomplishing any task.

- Uncharacteristically poor judgment — a person may make poor decisions which may lead to unrealistic involvement in activities, meetings and deadlines, reckless driving, spending sprees and foolish business ventures.

- Sustained period of behavior that is different from usual — a person may dress and/or act differently than he or she usually does, become a collector of various items, become indifferent to personal grooming, become obsessed with writing, or experience delusions.

- Unusual sexual drive.

- Abuse of drugs, particularly cocaine, alcohol or sleeping medications.

- Provocative, intrusive or aggressive behavior — a person may become enraged or paranoid if his or her grand ideas are stopped or excessive social plans are refused.

Symptoms of Depression

Some people experience periods of normal mood and behavior following a manic phase; however, the depressive phase will eventually appear. Symptoms of depression include:

- Persistent sad, anxious or empty mood

- Sleeping too much or too little, middle-of-the-night or early morning waking

- Reduced appetite and weight loss or increased appetite and weight gain

- Loss of interest or pleasure in activities, including sex

- Irritability or restlessness

- Difficulty concentrating, remembering or making decisions

- Fatigue or loss of energy

- Persistent physical symptoms that do not respond to treatment (such as chronic pain or digestive disorders)

- Thoughts of death or suicide, including suicide attempts (5)

No one should make a diagnosis on without consulting a professional psychiatrist. Diagnosing bipolar can be a complicated and difficult thing to do. I share this more extended list of symptoms so if you sense any type of problem that could be related to bipolar you can get the immediate help available.

There are a number of other mood disorders that cause children, adolescents and even adult's serious emotional problems. Often mood disorders of various types can be present in more than one person in a family. Usually most doctors and psychiatrists believe if one child has a mood disorder the odds are greater that another sibling will manifest symptoms. In our personal family our youngest son was diagnosed with ADHD in fourth grade.

Due to the frustration level with a person who has a mood disorder, they sometimes manifest something called Oppositional Defiant Disorder. We saw this tied in with bipolar and ADHD. I will include the symptoms of ODD and ADHD to give an overall picture of the challenges mood disorders present to individuals and families.

Children With Oppositional Defiant Disorder

All children are oppositional from time to time, particularly when tired, hungry, stressed or upset. They may argue, talk back, disobey, and defy parents, teachers, and other adults. Oppositional behavior is often a normal part of development for two to three year olds and early adolescents. However, openly uncooperative and hostile behavior becomes a serious concern when it is so frequent and consistent that it stands out when compared with other children of the same age and developmental level and when it affects the child's social, family, and academic life.

In children with Oppositional Defiant Disorder (ODD), there is an ongoing pattern of uncooperative, defiant, and hostile behavior toward authority figures that seriously interferes with the youngster's day to day functioning. Symptoms of ODD may include:

- Frequent temper tantrums
- Excessive arguing with adults
- Active defiance and refusal to comply with adult requests and rules
- Deliberate attempts to annoy or upset people
- Blaming others for his or her mistakes or misbehavior
- Often being touchy or easily annoyed by others
- Frequent anger and resentment
- Mean and hateful talking when upset
- Seeking revenge

The symptoms are usually seen in multiple settings, but may be more noticeable at home or at school. Five to fifteen percent of all school-age children have ODD. The causes of ODD are unknown, but many parents report that their child with ODD was more rigid and demanding than the child's siblings from an early age. Biological and environmental factors may have a role.

A child presenting with ODD symptoms should have a comprehensive evaluation. It is important to look for other disorders which may be present; such as, attention-deficit hyperactive disorder (ADHD), learning disabilities, mood disorders (depression, bipolar disorder) and anxiety disorders. It may be difficult to improve the symptoms of ODD without treating the coexisting disorder. Some children with ODD may go on to develop called conduct disorder.

Treatment of ODD may include: Parent Training Programs to help manage the child's behavior, Individual Psychotherapy to develop more effective anger management, Family Psychotherapy to improve communication, Cognitive-Behavioral Therapy to assist problem solving and decrease negativity, and Social Skills Training to increase flexibility and improve frustration tolerance with peers.

A child with ODD can be very difficult for parents. These parents need support and understanding. Parents can help their child with ODD in the following ways:

- Always build on the positives, give the child praise and positive reinforcement when he shows flexibility or cooperation.
- Take a time-out or break if you are about to make the conflict with your child worse, not better. This is good modeling for your child. Support your child if he decides to take a time-out to prevent overreacting.

- Pick your battles. Since the child with ODD has trouble avoiding power struggles, prioritize the things you want your child to do. If you give your child a time-out in his room for misbehavior, don't add time for arguing. Say "your time will start when you go to your room."
- Set up reasonable, age appropriate limits with consequences that can be enforced consistently.
- Maintain interests other than your child with ODD, so that managing your child doesn't take all your time and energy. Try to work with and obtain support from the other adults (teachers, coaches, and spouse) dealing with your child.
- Manage your own stress with exercise and relaxation. Use respite care as needed.

Many children with ODD will respond to the positive parenting techniques. Parents may ask their pediatrician or family physician to refer them to a child and adolescent psychiatrist, who can diagnose and treat ODD and any coexisting psychiatric condition.

Children Who Can't Pay Attention /ADHD

Parents are distressed when they receive a note from school saying that their child won't listen to the teacher or causes trouble in class. One possible reason for this kind of behavior is Attention Deficit Hyperactivity Disorder (ADHD).

Even though the child with ADHD often wants to be a good student, the impulsive behavior and difficulty paying attention in class frequently interferes and causes problems. Teachers, parents, and friends know that the child is misbehaving or different but they may not be able to tell exactly what is wrong.

Any child may show inattention, distractibility, impulsivity, or hyperactivity at times, but the child with ADHD shows these symptoms and behaviors more frequently and severely than other children of the same age or developmental level. ADHD occurs in 3-5% of school age children. ADHD must begin before the age of seven and it can continue into adulthood. ADHD runs in families with about 25% of biological parents also having this medical condition.

A child with ADHD often shows some of the following:

- Trouble paying attention
- Inattention to details and makes careless mistakes easily distracted
- Loses school supplies, forgets to turn in homework
- Trouble finishing class work and homework
- Trouble listening
- Trouble following multiple adult commands
- Blurts out answers
- Impatience
- Fidgets or squirms
- Leaves seat and runs about or climbs excessively
- Seems "on the go"
- Talks too much and has difficulty playing quietly
- Interrupts or intrudes on others

A child presenting with ADHD symptoms should have a comprehensive evaluation. Parents should ask their pediatrician or family physician to refer them to a child and adolescent psychiatrist, who can diagnose and treat this medical condition. A child with ADHD may also have other psychiatric disorders such as conduct disorder, anxiety disorder, depressive disorder, or bipolar disorder. These children may also have learning disabilities.

Without proper treatment, the child may fall behind in schoolwork, and friendships may suffer. The child experiences more failure than success and is criticized by teachers and family who do not recognize a health problem.

Research clearly demonstrates that medication can help improve attention, focus, goal directed behavior, and organizational skills. Medications most likely to be helpful include the stimulants (various methylphenidate and amphetamine preparations) and the non-stimulant, atomoxetine. Other medications such as guanfacine, clonidine, and some antidepressants may also be helpful.

Other treatment approaches may include cognitive-behavioral therapy, social skills training, parent education, and modifications to the child's education program. Behavioral therapy can help a child control aggression, modulate social behavior, and be more productive. Cognitive therapy can help child build self-esteem, reduce negative thoughts, and improve problem-solving skills. Parents can learn management skills such as issuing instructions one-step at a time rather than issuing multiple requests at once. Education modifications can address ADHD symptoms along with any coexisting learning disabilities.

A child who is diagnosed with ADHD and treated appropriately can have a productive and successful life. (6)

Correctly diagnosing and effectively dealing with a mood disorder is very difficult and not something to be taken lightly. If you feel you or someone you love may have symptoms of a mood disorder be sure to seek out medical help from your primary doctor and ask for professional psychiatric referrals.

Do not put it off if you have any symptoms whatsoever. Finally don't diagnose yourself, a loved one or a friend simply by reading the symptoms in this chapter.

Kenneth Dignan

Chapter Ten

Amazing Grace
Transparent Honesty

I have tried to be transparently honest as I show the pain and sorrow my son and my family have felt. We are imperfect, frail, and sinful because we are human. We need a loving God who offers us hope, forgiveness, and eternal life by His grace.

God's Amazing Grace

Some have asked me, "Do I believe my son is definitely in heaven?" To that I answer, "Most definitely." As you've seen, our son was in serious mental confusion and unable to think correctly. Still I believe the grace of God was exhibited. God's grace covers the unborn that die from abortions, children who die before the age of accountability, those with Down syndrome and cognitive disabilities, many with mental illnesses and the like. God will always do what is right for those who have a genuine mental disorder or disease. Some mental problems present a big difficulty to make a sincere and realistic confession of faith, when presented with the claims of Christ. There are many who struggle beyond their abilities and spiritual understanding to deal with destructive and sinful habits.

God's grace means unmerited favor. Blessings you have not earned or do not deserve.

Do Not Give Up On God

I hope and pray any of you who personally have or know a relative who has a chemical imbalance or mental disorder will not give up on God. He loves you and desires to be with you no matter what.

Even though it may be hard to accept at times, I am confident God allowed Ryan to go through what he did. Not because He likes to see people make wrong choices or become mentally ill or addicted to substances. But the God who creates us knows that tragedy, accidents, illnesses, war, pain, and death are all a part of this life. And God uses everything to accomplish His divine purposes that go beyond the human ability to understand. The only way anything will make sense is if we look at the things in our lives through the eyes of eternity. What might look terrible in this life will be arranged by God to bring heavenly glory when seen on the other side of eternity.

In the end, God saved Ryan by allowing him to come home to heaven, where he had no more pain or confusion. I believe Ryan didn't really kill himself; he was trying to kill his pain. As wrong and terrible as suicide is, I've come to see when someone has a serious mental disorder and unable to think clearly and sanely, strange as it may be, suicide, to them appears to be the only solution. Dr. Kay Redfield Jamison has said, "Suicide is a permanent solution for a temporary problem." But the one who is hurting does not believe their pain is temporary. A fog of depression clouds their mind making it impossible to believe things will get better.

Whatever you are going through if you have a mood disorder realize life is hard. Be open to spiritual possibilities. Do all you can to accept the fact that therapy, medicines and faith can help you live a productive and meaningful life. You might be surprised at what insight can come your way if you venture beyond this earthly realm of existence and remain open to the spiritual realm tapped in the Bible.

More Research Needed

A tremendous amount of work still needs to be done to broaden public awareness of mood disorders like bipolar. A lot of money is being raised for AIDS, Cancer, Muscular Dystrophy, Multiple Sclerosis, Parkinson's, ALS and other serious diseases. Yet more studies need to be undertaken on behalf of mood disorders and mental illnesses.

We stand at the precipice of a mountain that needs to be climbed on behalf of individuals like my son Ryan.

Father Rubey

Father Charles T. Rubey, founder of the LOSS program, wrote: "As survivors struggle with survivor issues, one of the gnawing questions that are asked is how someone could commit an act like suicide knowing the impact that their death was going to have on the survivor?"

"A person who takes their life doesn't perceive the shattering of a family system on account of their suicide. Their act is not an act of selfishness. Their act is not cowardly. Their act is an act performed by someone who is incapable of perceiving the ramifications of a suicide. It is difficult to understand depression unless we have been there. It is impossible to calculate the paralysis that comes over a person who is suffering from depression or other forms of mental illness.

The mind has suffered a stroke and the mind becomes paralyzed. This paralysis is focused on one thing and one thing only--to get out of the pain, and the only way out of the pain is suicide. The mind has become paralyzed in very much the same way that a limb can become paralyzed because of a trauma or because of a stroke. We can understand a spinal cord injury causing a person to become a paraplegic. We can understand a person suffering a stroke and losing the use of an arm or a leg. Think of mental illness causing the same type of paralysis, but not on a back, or an arm, or a leg or a neck, but on one's mind. This is the effect and impact of mental illness on the mind. It has paralyzed the mind and the mind is capable only of focusing on suicide as a way out of the paralysis." (1)

This is a hard statement to grasp and accept, but makes a lot of sense. I know our son would not have ended his life unless something went terribly wrong with his mind. He had to be suffering from a truly debilitating illness.

What Else Could We Have Done?

My wife and I keep thinking maybe there were more things we could have done to help prevent his suicide. Maybe if we would have gotten him another dog after his beloved mini-Dachshund, Spanky, died, it could have made him feel better. Maybe if we didn't have a basement we would have heard him walking around that night. We should have disposed of the rope on the weight set in our basement.

Father Rubey's statement brings some peace of mind. Ryan was a confused, sick person and in his illness he knew of no other way to deal with his pain and suffering. Chemical imbalances in the brain, terminal sicknesses, chronic pain, and various suffering can bring a person to commit drastic acts.

A Caring E-mail

A few days after my son's death, I received a moving e-mail from a high school student who attended the church where I am a pastor:

> *I heard about the loss and I cannot even imagine what you guys are felling. I can, however, relate to what your son was feeling before he took his life. I really feel that God was telling me to write you this E-mail and I hope you will be encouraged by what I have to say. What I am about to tell you has changed a lot of people's lives.*
>
> *When I was in seventh grade, my family was falling apart and I hated myself.*
>
> *I felt hopeless. I started cutting myself and I had numerous eating disorders.*
>
> *I have been in and out of hospitals and have seen so many counselors throughout my life, but nothing worked. I was just filled with more and more anger and sadness. I started actually listening to you and others in the church.*

That's when my life started to change. I stopped the drugs and drinking, and my life is now clean. I now do not mind baring the scars on my arms, legs, and stomach. I tell people they are my battle scars. I have won the battle, and believe it or not, you helped me.

Pastor Ken, I want you to know that you are a hero to me and many other people including your sons. I know that in my heart. I need you and your family to believe that none of this was your fault. There was nothing that could be done.

I know from being suicidal that no matter what anyone says, it does not change your thoughts. So, please do not feel like you guys have failed. Do not feel that there was anything you could have said to make Ryan change his mind.

Everything happens for a reason. This tragedy is terrible and I know that your family's lives are changed forever. Think about it this way, though. This loss may change other people's lives forever. For every bad thing that happens, I truly believe with all my heart that more good comes out of it. People's lives will be changed forever when they hear the story of Ryan. I wish he could be here to see how people could be led to Christ through him.

Even though he is not here on earth to witness, he will be watching from up above. God had a special place made for him. It may be hard to see that there is light ahead; I promise you there is, though. You do not know how much of an effect you have made on my life. Seeing how strong you were and how deep your faith was has helped me plant my faith, and you have changed my life in more ways than I can describe.

Please remember that no matter what happens God will bring you through it.

His shoulder is always there to cry on and He will listen to you no matter what time of the day. Stay strong. I love you all.

Notes like this have helped sustain my family and me through our painful loss. In times of great trial and hurt, we have received the support and love of others. It is amazing to experience the compassion of family, friends, neighbors, and a church congregation.

Ryan is Safe

Ryan is now safe with God, yet we here on earth struggle to come to grips with all that happened. We miss him greatly.

People still ask us how we are doing implying, Are you over your son's death yet? Are you feeling better now? I know they mean well and they are just trying to show concern. Granted, as time goes by, the tears and raw emotions do subside a bit and you experience longer times of emotional stability.

But there are still days when out of the blue, thoughts about your loved one hit you like a tornado. You miss them so much you can hardly take it.

When you lose a loved one, especially to suicide, it is a pain you must learn to bear. You will never get over it. You will always think about them.

The apostle Paul asked God to remove a painful thorn in his flesh. God said no. "My grace will give you sufficient strength to bear up under it. My power is made perfect in you through your weaknesses." (2Corinthians 12:7-11) I paraphrase this scripture verse.

Most of us hope for as many years on this earth as possible, but what really matters is how you live your years. Making an impact on others should matter most. I can proudly say Ryan's life was full because he touched so many with his brightness. I wrote a poem titled "What I miss most about my son."

WHAT I MISS MOST ABOUT MY SON
By Ken Dignan

Ryan, I miss watching you walk around the house and anxiously looking out the garage door for your friends.

I miss listening to music with you and talking about the sound and words.

I miss seeing you in your black leather jacket.

I miss you helping me up from my recliner. You helped me up from that chair better than anyone. (In fact, I haven't sat in it since you left).

I miss eating lunch with you. Eating with you and talking about food was great fun.

I miss seeing you play with your dog, Spanky.

I miss seeing you interact with your brothers and your mom when you were in a good mood. You could show such a warm and caring heart.

I miss driving around with you in my van.

I loved watching you wrestle with every ounce of strength you had.

I loved watching you play football with the Bolingbrook Trojans, Orland Pioneers and the Sandburg High School football team. It was a thrill to see you give 110% effort on every play.

I loved coaching you in baseball and basketball.

I loved seeing you study hard and get great grades.

I loved seeing you have many friends who came over to the house and constantly called on the phone.

I loved watching movies with you and talking about them.

I loved talking with you about spiritual things. (God, Jesus, and the Bible)

I loved seeing you and your mother give each other back rubs, and tickle each other as you sat on the couch.

I loved seeing you interact with your cousins and other little kids. You loved kids a lot.

You were one of my best friends, and it was a privilege and an honor to be your father. I'm sorry you had to leave so soon. I'm looking forward to seeing you in heaven as soon as I get there. Say hi to Jesus for me.

Miss you, Pops (As he often called me)

My wife, Joni, wrote a beautiful poem about our son shortly after he died:

Holding Ryan
<u>By Joni Dignan</u>

Etched in my heart forever is his entrance into my life. Only five hours of labor for such a son as he, worth so many more.

I was in awe as I held him. As he grew, holding onto Ryan became more difficult.

He was up a tree, or under a bed, or at the park, or building a GI Joe fort almost anywhere.

I had to catch him to hold him. I thanked God for this amazing boy.

He was an intense student who did his homework the minute he came home from school so he could go outside and play with his brothers and friends. Sleepovers and sports filled his nights and weekends. Still I held on, trying to make sure he followed the right path. I was so glad God gave him to me.

High school came and he started pulling away from my arms. It was all I could do to touch him with my fingers as he raced out the door, urgent to succeed, eager to experience life, anxious to discover who he was.

He would come and hold me once in a while, and I would hang on for dear life, feeling his rock-hard frame almost squeeze my breath away.

Then one morning, Ryan was gone.

I held him one more time, but he didn't respond. Now I hold him in my heart; I hug his memory close.

My only comfort is knowing God is holding Ryan whenever He can catch him as he runs through heaven, playing Frisbee golf with the angels.

Our home seems smaller at times since Ryan died. He could be bigger than life and make a lot of noise. But now, in his absence, the quiet is deafening and painful. Many nights his memory cuts my heart like a knife. We await our reunion with fond expectation on the other side of eternity.

Time Goes On

Almost three years have passed since I began to write this story about what Ryan and our family went through up until his passing and thereafter. When Christmas 2004 passed I came across a letter Joni wrote to Ryan. I conclude this book with her letter.

Dear Ryan, I spent another Christmas away from you. Through all the laughter, presents and snacks, thoughts of you floated through my mind. Your smile, your love, and even the last few years of your life, that brought us all such pain. I miss you, Ry.

You were my one-of-a-kind boy, a particular joy to me. I am talking to a counselor about you and she encourages me to remember the good times. Of which there are so many. When the veil of sorrow lifts from time to time, when the regret of losing you subsides for a moment, I am blessed by a golden memory here and there. That wonderful day when your kindergarten teacher, Ms. R, told me you could stay home with me another year. The time we spent at the antique village in Richmond, IL, looking at old knives and eating ice cream cones. How you would stick your arm over mine and I knew to start tickling, especially your hands. And the late night back scratching so you could sleep, I long to have them back.

Your belongings are dwindling here, your bed was disposed of, and your clothes fill only two boxes. People don't talk about you as much; uncertain if that would bring us relief or pain. Your friends don't call.

We had our second concert in your honor for bipolar awareness, suicide prevention and of course, to remember you and help bring your story out so that other kids like you can know they aren't alone. Your pictures are being readied for framing, if I ever get that done. Somehow it is still very difficult to look at your face.

I miss you too much. But I know you are happy where you are, in Heaven, with God. Your pain is gone, and you are who you were intended to be – forever, happy, generous, sensitive, so fun loving.

I can imagine: you racing with Jason (his cousin who died at age twelve from an accident) through Heaven, stopping to give Grandma and Grandpa St John (her parents) a kiss now and then, and Jesus smiling at you.

Merry Christmas up there Ryan, You were my blessing here for a while. Now you are my hope of eternity. I can't wait to see you.

Love, Mom

Resource Quotes per Chapter

Chapter One

1- The Strong Willed Child and Dare to Discipline-By Dr. James Dobson, Tyndale House Publishers.

2- Website, themoodyones.com

3- ESPN Cable Sports Network

4- Barret Robbins Article written by Mark Emmons, San Jose Mercury News in California, January 19, 2005. Contact Mark Emmons at memmons@mercury news.com.

Chapter Two

American Psychiatric Association. Diagnostic and Statistical Manual for Mental Disorders, fourth edition (DSM-IV). Washington, DC: American Psychiatric Press, 1994.

Chapter Three

1   Schizophrenia and Bipolar Disorders: A Family Manual-By Dr. Wagemaker

2   Ibid.

3   Depression.com, Dr. Kathleen Brady, M.D. 1996

4 His Bright Light, The Story of Nick Traina, author Danielle Steel.

Chapter Five

1- Dr. Wagemaker, Ibid. p.38

2- Out of the Nightmare, author David L. Conry, Ph.D

3- Night Falls Fast, author Kay Redfield Jamison M.D.

Chapter Six

1- Quotations from the New International Version of the Bible and The New King James Version.

2- Words to He's My Son written by Mark Schultz, BMI

Chapter Seven

1- Romans 8:28

2- Grieving a Suicide by Albert Y. Hsu, IVP.

Chapter Nine

1- All resources from websites of various health organizations listed at the end of the book..

2- The Jed Foundation – 583 Broadway, Suite 8B New York, NY 10012

3-The National Institute of Mental Health

4-The National Mental Health Association, Signs and Symptoms of Bipolar Disorder.

5-Facts for Families© information sheets are developed, owned and distributed by the American

Academy of Child and Adolescent Psychiatry (AACAP). Hard copies of Facts sheets may be reproduced for personal or educational use without written permission, but cannot be included in material presented for sale or profit. All Facts can be viewed and printed from the AACAP website (www.aacap.org). Facts sheets many not be reproduced, duplicated or posted on any other Internet website without written consent from AACAP. Organizations are permitted to create links to AACAP's website and specific Facts sheets. To purchase complete sets of Facts for Families, please contact the AACAP Circulation Clerk at 800.333.7636, ext. 131.

Chapter Ten
1- The Oblelisk, Newsletter of LOSS (Loving Outreach to Survivors of Suicide), Chicago, IL

Kenneth Dignan

Bibliography

Conroy, David L. OUT OF THE NIGHTMARE. Recovery from Depression and Suicidal Pain. New York: New Liberty Press, 1991.

Bruce, James W III. FROM GRIEF TO GLORY. Wheaton, IL: Crossway Books, 2002.

Wagemaker, Herbert M.D. with Buchholz, Ann. SCHIZOPHRENIA AND BIPOLAR DISORDERS (often misdiagnosed often mistreated). A Family Manual. Ponte Vedra Beach, FL: Ponte Vedra Publishing, 1999.

Hsu, Albert Y. Grieving a Suicide. A Loved One's Search for Comfort, Answers & Hope. Downers Grove, IL: Intervarsity Press, 2002.

Kent, Carol. When I lay My Isaac Down. Colorado Springs, CO: NavPress, 2004.

Jamison, Kay Redfield. Night Falls Fast. Understanding Suicide. New York: Alfred A Knopf, 1999.

Jamison, Kay Redfield. An Unquiet Mind. New York: Alfred A. Knopf, 1996.

Miklowitz, David J. The Bipolar Disorder Survival Guide. New York / London. The Guilford Press. 2002.

Steel, Danielle. His Bright Light. The Story of Nick Traina. New York: Delacorte Press, 1998.

Reference Contacts

References For More Information (Many quotes are taken from these sources)

National Institute of Mental Health (NIMH)
Office of Communications
6001 Executive Boulevard, Room 8184, MSC 9663
Bethesda, MD 20892-9663
Phone: 301-443-4513 or 1-866-615-NIMH (6464), toll-free
TTY: 301-443-8431; FAX: 301-443-4279
FAX 4U: 301-443-5158
E-mail: nimhinfo@nih.gov
Web site: http://www.nimh.nih.gov

American Association of Suicidology
Phone: 202-237-2280
Web site: http://www.suicidology.org

American Foundation for Suicide Prevention
Phone: 212-363-3500
Web site: http://www.afsp.org

National Hopeline Network
Phone: 1-800-SUICIDE (1-800-784-2433)

Toll Free, 24 hour crisis hotline

Suicide Prevention Advocacy Network
Phone: 770-998-8819
Web site: http://www.spanusa.org

For more information on Bipolar or referrals for local service contact your local mental health association or:

NMHA Resource Center
National Mental Health Association
2001 North Beauregard Street, 12th Floor
Alexandria, VA 22311
Phone: 800-969-6642 (NMHA)
TTY: 800-433-5959
www.nmha.org

The Jason Foundation, Inc.
181 East Main Street • Jefferson Bldg. • Suite 5
Hendersonville, TN 37075

The Jed Foundation
583 Broadway • Suite 8B
New York, NY 10012
Phone: 212-647-7544
Fax: 212-343-1141
emailus@jedfoundation.org

American Association of Suicidology
5221 Wisconsin Avenue, NW
Washington, DC 20015
Phone: (202) 237-2280
Fax: (202) 237-2282

Ken's Personal Biography

Ken Dignan has been a credentialed minister since 1976. He has a varied background in Christianity having been raised a Roman Catholic, becoming a "Born Again" Christian at 20 years of age. He then received a B.A. in Bible from North Central University in Minneapolis, MN; an M.A. in Biblical Studies from The Assemblies of God Theological Seminary in Springfield, MO; and a Th.D. in Theology from Carolina University of Theology (Independent Baptist) in Belmont NC.

He has served in a pastoral capacity at Maranatha Chapel, Evergreen Park, IL; First Assembly in Jerseyville, IL; Living Water Community Church, Bolingbrook, IL; The Stone Church, Palos Heights, IL and currently the Pastor of Eagle Rock Community Church, Orland Park, IL.

He has hosted a Contemporary Christian radio show called "The Christian Alternative" in the St. Louis area and currently serves as the Executive Producer and host of a weekly 30-minute television program called "Ken Dignan, From the Heart," seen on the Total Living Network, Comcast Chicagoland and FamilyNet nationally. Ken is the Founder of "Til Healing Comes Ministries" and "The Ryan Dignan Association, a subsidiary of THCM.

He is the author of "Til Healing Comes." He has recorded a vocal CD of gospel worship music; has been a guest speaker for a Joni & Friends Family Camp, a guest class lecturer for Moody Bible Institute in Chicago, and spoken in over 100 churches throughout the country since 1991.

To contact the author:

Rev. Kenneth M. Dignan
P. O. Box 816
Orland Park, IL 60462
kdignan@aol.com

Ken Dignan is available for speaking engagements and personal appearances. For more information contact the publisher at:

ADVANTAGE BOOKS™
PO Box 160847
Altamonte Springs, FL 32716

To order additional copies of this book or to see a complete list of all **ADVANTAGE BOOKS™** visit our online bookstore at:

www.advbookstore.com

or call our toll free order number at: 1-888-383-3110

Longwood, Florida, USA

"we bring dreams to life"™
www.advbooks.com

CPSIA information can be obtained at www.ICGtesting.com
Printed in the USA
LVOW061628010912

296966LV00001B/7/A